AVOIDING
IT DISASTERS

ISBN 978-1-7753575-0-6

Ordering Information:
Quantity sales. Special discounts are available on quantity purchases by corporations, associations, and others. For details, email requests to special_sales@thinkingworks.com

Typesetting and Cover Design by FormattingExperts.com

AVOIDING
IT DISASTERS

Fallacies about enterprise systems
and how you can rise above them

Lance Gutteridge, Ph.D.

*I dedicate this book to all the people who
have been harmed by enterprise software systems;
you deserve better*

*In theory there is no difference
between theory and practice, in practice there is.*

—Yogi Berra

1
INTRODUCTION

Susan[1] waited anxiously for an important mail delivery as she had done for the previous month. She was hoping that a paycheck she had been owed for more than six months would slide through the mail slot. She and her husband needed the money badly. Her husband had been laid off from his construction job and they had burned through most of their savings. They were already late on the mortgage and the bank has sent them a letter demanding payment. They had decided that her husband would go back to school but they needed to put down the first installment of the fees. It was an extremely stressful time.

When the mail came she grabbed it from the box and leafed through the few items. Just an offer from a car dealership, a letter to a previous occupant, and a flyer from a local supermarket. Not a sign of the paycheck she had been hoping to see. She had worked hard all summer and her employer still hadn't paid her.

Her heart sank. Her husband would have to cancel his registration and take a low-paying job at a fast food outlet.

But they lived in Vancouver, Canada. Surely an employer couldn't get away with not paying its employees?

---

[1] I have mostly avoided any real names of people or still-existing organizations in this book. This is because the circumstances around system failure are seldom flattering and it is not my goal to hold people up to ridicule for things that are, for the most part, not their fault or out of their control. All the stories are based on real-life incidents. In some cases, I have simplified the circumstances to make a clearer point.

In Canada people who don't get paid can seek help from the employment standards branch of the provincial government. In British Columbia the government, as in all Canadian provinces, has strict laws about paying employees and the enforcement officials have powerful tools that enable them to force delinquent employers to pay the wages they owe.

The responsibility to pay employees is taken very seriously in Canada. So much so that directors of companies are personally liable for unpaid wages. Directors of large companies routinely take out insurance to make sure they are not bankrupted by their obligation to make good on wages owed to a large group of employees.

So how was it that Susan's employer has not been paying a large segment of its workforce, and paying wrong amounts to another whole group of employees? And doing this to thousands of employees for three years in some cases?

How can they get away with this?

Well, Susan's employer was not some shifty fly-by-night operation—it was the Canadian Federal Government. The reason she wasn't paid wasn't that the government was out of funds or that it was trying to cheat her out of wages she had earned. It was a result of their new computerized payroll system, called Phoenix.

Susan was not alone. The Canadian Government employs over 300,000 people, ranging from full-time civil servants to temporary workers, and over 70,000 of them had been underpaid or not paid at all. Another large group had been overpaid and were worried about what they should do with the extra money and how to give it back.

By 2018 this had been going on for three years, and despite assurance from the minister in charge, there seemed to be no sign of it being corrected any time soon. In the spring budget the government, tired of all the complaints and demonstrations, announced it was terminating the project and would look for another solution.[2]

The problem started when the previous Conservative government was trying to cut spending by improving efficiency in the administration of the civil service. Like a lot of organizations, they were seduced by the thought of implementing a new software system that would, as they were told by the software salespeople, move the entire payroll operation to one location and save significant operational costs.

IBM came calling with a proposal to use an Oracle payroll system that could be adapted to meet the Canadian Government's particular situation. If the government had checked they would have discovered that the system had caused a total disaster in the state of Queensland in Australia, resulting in a billion-dollar lawsuit. The Queensland government lost that case, which showed that IBM was certainly much better at writing contracts and defending against lawsuits than it was at writing software. The same software had been implemented in Palm Beach, Florida with disastrous results, similarly for the Police Department in Austin, Texas where it failed to properly pay the police officers. In Austin this resulted in a precipitous drop in morale and some rumors of resulting suicides.

According to recent media reports the Canadian government did not check the history of this software and was unaware of those past problems. The current results have been similar to the past experiences: hundreds of millions of dollars spent to acquire the system, hundreds

---

[2] I have not put links into all the articles on the Phoenix payroll system. There are so many that it would fill an entire book. Just search for 'phoenix payroll problems Canada' or anything similar, and you will get over 10 pages of links to articles detailing the problems.

of millions more to modify it, and more millions draining out to try to actually make it work. Meanwhile, tens of thousands of employees have been not paid, tens of thousands have been underpaid and tens of thousands more overpaid. This has forced some civil servants to cash in retirement savings, forced some to cancel education plans, and inflicted stress on the most vulnerable—those who depend on government pension checks.

This is quite shocking, especially as it concerns such a large and credible organization as the Canadian Federal Government. However, it is perhaps not the worst example of system failure. In the U.S.A., various jurisdictions have used the Odyssey system for processing court dates, criminal records, and sentences. Problems with this system have resulted in innocent people being incarcerated.

It is bad enough to not be paid by your employer but imagine losing your liberty because of a system failure.

In the early 1960s there was a short story "Computers Don't Argue" by Gordon R. Dickson.[3] Presented as a series of letters, it starts out when a member of a book club tries to return a copy of Kidnapped by Robert Louis Stevenson that has been sent to him because of a computer error. They ignore his letters and take him to court when he doesn't pay the cost of the book. Another computer error causes him to be charged with the kidnapping of Robert Louis Stevenson, which the computers change to kidnap-murder when they discover that Robert Louis Stevenson is dead. He is sentenced to death, but the governor finally applies some common sense and pardons him. Unfortunately, the pardon is rejected by the computer systems, as it didn't have the right authorization code, and the poor consumer is executed anyway.

---

[3] I don't know if this is still in print but there is a Wikipedia article on it at https://en.wikipedia.org/wiki/Computers_Don%27t_Argue

It was a great story, but when I read it I thought it was implausible. At the time I was one of a very small number of people who had even programmed a computer (the number of programmers at the time was probably less than 100,000). I didn't believe that humans would ever delegate judicial authority to a computer system. Surely there would always be a human to exercise common sense?

But at that time, I was inexperienced. I thought that all human problems were solvable by technology. What can I say—I was young. I hadn't yet observed that when humans have automated large flows of data it is impossible to check everything. The Odyssey system shows that the story was perhaps not as fantastic as I thought, and somewhat prescient.

If you have been involved in the selection, installation, or use of a computer system in an organization, you have almost certainly experienced the frustration and cost of enterprise system problems. Things like: reports that are inaccurate or just not available, system failures at the worst possible times, or the embarrassment of having to tell an important client that they were accidentally overcharged. These are problems that business people face all the time. They have become so common that they are just not noteworthy. Before computers these problems would have been shocking and people would have been disciplined, if not outright fired, on grounds of incompetence.

Those days of stricter accountability are over. Today system failure is a dreary fact of life. For the failure of an enterprise system to gain the attention of the mainstream media in the second decade of the 21st century it almost certainly has to be one costing over 100 million dollars, and preferably over a billion. And there are no organizations that are immune. Governments, not-for-profits, small businesses, and large international corporations are all subject to the ravages of system failure.

There is no real way of determining the yearly cost to the world economy of enterprise system failure. You can look on the Internet and see estimates as high as 6 trillion dollars per year. Given that much of the cost is incurred by organizations that are reluctant to make their problems public, there are no reliable statistics that analysts can base an estimate on. The fact that you can see credible industry commentators claiming losses in the trillions shows that the actual numbers are almost certainly a measurable percentage of the planet's economic activity.

What is going on? Are these systems so complicated that failure is a necessary companion to the benefits they undoubtedly bring to modern corporations? Because as frustrating and damaging as system failure can be, no one would seriously try to run an organization of any size without the help of computers and without some kind of automated system to produce the necessary financial and management reports.

Is this all there is? Must we tolerate this level of failure, with this amount of disruption to every part of our lives? Will this still be the case 10 years from now, 20 years from now? At the start of the 22nd century are we still going to be reading media articles (or watching 3D floating holograms) about yet another large system failure, about how someone was wrongfully incarcerated by computer problems, and about some organization having a payroll disaster that they can't seem to fix?

Yet you read about great software successes—stories of amazing software that translates languages, beats the world's champion at the game of Go, and guides robots rolling around on the surface of Mars. So maybe you have wondered whether system failure is something unique to your organization—are other organizations somehow better? Are they succeeding in software where you are failing?

This book will answer these questions for you. I will show you why your common sense, a human heritage of hundreds of thousands of years of operating in the physical world, can mislead you when it comes to making software decisions. I will show you the real story behind the scenes, the things that programmers know but have failed to communicate to the wider world. I will show you what is wrong with the way enterprise systems are being built, and then I will give you some tools to counter the software salespeople and their claims, so you can be more in control when dealing with software acquisition. I will finish by looking ahead to what I believe has to happen to return a level of sanity to this broken but entirely essential industry, and what I believe the future of enterprise computing will look like.

This is the information you need to operate in this perilous world, a world where the very survival of your organization can be in danger, a world where huge monies can be extracted from you with very little to show in return, and a world that has been built to serve the needs of the suppliers at the expense of you the customer.

Come with me on an exploration—an exploration of an industry like no other. An exploration that follows my own journey, a journey from wide-eyed teenager who learned programming in a university mathematics course in 1963, through to being an owner-partner of a 55-person software company, and currently an architect of a tool designed to allow business people to construct their own business logic. During that journey I learned that programming was a good skill to have and a reliable source of income, but I also learned that there was much more to this industry than the technical side. I learned that there was also a dark side where people could use pretend knowledge to further their own ends at the expense of others and where system failures could spread havoc in organizations and people's lives.

A lot of managers feel insecure around software and information technology staff. Anxious not to show ignorance, they try to avoid software issues and let someone else handle them. That's fine if they have someone trustworthy and capable, but in many cases this willful blindness can leave solutions up to outside consultants and those consultants may make decisions based on their own interests and agendas.

Systems are an integral part of any business and will grow even more so going forward. To try not to think about them, hoping the problems will solve themselves, will not work. So what knowledge do you need to understand what is going on with enterprise systems? This book will give you that knowledge and explain why all these systems are failing.

I will show you what is really going on, why these systems are failing so often, and what you can do about it. I will show you that the root cause of all this is a simple but powerful property that is the most important difference between the physical world and the world of software.

I have kept everything in the language of business. It is not my intent to baffle you with techno-babble so that you feel inferior and won't ask awkward questions. One of the things about all of this technology is that at its roots it is not that complicated. You don't need to have any specialized knowledge other than the general computer knowledge that all of us need to be in business in these first decades of the 21st century. As we shall see, most of these problems are the result of the very human propensity to try to fit new things into old patterns. When you start to see what the real patterns should be I think you will see software and software disasters, in a different, more revealing light.

2
WHERE ARE WE?

It was a Monday morning in August of 1970. I was working on my Ph.D. in computability theory and had been working summers at a large pulp and paper company. I had been a programmer in their operations research department for the last five summers. I was in a hurry because I had been away for a week at a mathematics conference and I was anxious to finish a simulation program I had been working on. I took the stairs two at a time to the eleventh floor as it was faster than waiting for an elevator, and besides I was 23 and liked the challenge. Sweaty and panting I burst out of the stairwell door and took my usual short cut through the accounting department, weaving in and out of desks until I turned the corner into the Operations Research department.

It was empty.

There was no one there and everything had been cleared off the desks in the common area. I checked the offices. All of them, including my manager's office, were empty except for overflowing wastebaskets.

I was stunned to find out that no one I worked with was there. The programmers were gone, my manager was gone, his manager was gone. All of them had been laid off the week before. No one there really knew who I was. They recognized me as that kid (I was 23 but could have passed for 15) they had seen around, but they had no idea of what I did or why I was there. I stood there, totally confused. The whole situation was surreal.

Once I got over the initial shock I tried to figure out what to do. Luckily, I had a purchase order. The Operations Research department had purchased my services as they would purchase paper or erasers. I met with the company lawyer, who was bemused by the situation and studied my PO. I had prepared a list of what I had been paid so far and what was remaining out of the total amount. They paid out the remaining balance (the grand sum, as I remember it, was $700). Given that my rent at university housing was around $130 a month, it was enough money to allow me to complete the summer before my teaching position started in the fall.

I didn't know it at the time but this event was not going to prove to be that unusual. The high-tech industry in general and the software sector in particular, has always been in a state of disruption. Companies collapse, projects are canceled, and departments are dissolved. Over my career I found out that this was just the nature of the business.

My summer job had started several years before. I had been working as a shipping clerk for 90 cents an hour, and just before that I had been fired as a gardener (I didn't really know weeds from flowers and had a bad run of guessing). The previous year at university I had taken a course in numerical analysis, and in the first part of the course they taught us computer programming so we could do the calculations. At the beginning of the summer I registered at the government employment office (in those days it actually found you summer jobs). I realized that if I was categorized as a shipping clerk that was the only kind of job I would get, so I registered as a management trainee, mentioning that I had programming skills. To my surprise I got a programming job with a large forestry company that operated pulp mills and saw mills all over the province. It harvested wood from massive areas, some of which were larger than most European countries.

The person who hired me was Dr. S., a Welsh Ph.D. who was an expert in Operations Research (OR). OR was developed during WWII as a scientific approach to several real-world problems. In wartime they were problems such as determining an optimal pattern of depth charges to maximize the probability of destroying a submarine that was detected at a location and had moved in an unknown direction. In peacetime these kinds of mathematical techniques were applied to business problems such as minimizing the costs of feed blending while maintaining nutritional requirements.

Dr. S. convinced the management of the forestry company that these techniques could be applied to harvesting wood for pulp and lumber. The company's areas (called Tree Farm Licenses or TFLs) could be divided into smaller areas, each one categorized by their species mix (fir, larch, birch, etc.), each of which had different characteristics for pulp manufacturing. A cost of logging could be assigned to each of these areas. The computer could run a technique called Linear Programming and come up with a plan that would find the smallest cost that could generate the target revenue.

I helped construct the equations and punch them into cards. Some days I would take a four-foot-long metal tray with thousands of punched cards clamped into it, to the only computer in town, an IBM 7040 at UBC (University of British Columbia). It seemed like a giant machine in those days, and it was, at least in physical size. It consisted of massive tape drives, multiple cabinets the size of industrial refrigerators, and a console with flashing lights and lots of switches. However, in terms of memory and the speed of its processor, it wouldn't even come close to the least powerful cell phone you can buy today. Our computer runs would be done at night when the computer was available, and they took from four to six hours to complete. I would play chess with the night operator on the small table that IBM had conveniently built into the console.

It was an interesting way to start my career, but even at the start I had some misgivings about the value of the calculations.

Dr. S. had sold this approach to the management of the company. These were rough-talking, hard-drinking, cigar-smoking kind of guys (yes—they were all men in that era) who had started their careers on the green chain or even cutting down giant trees with chain saws. His fast-talking patter must have sounded like double-dutch to them and I know that none of them really understood the approach. But as I was to learn time and time again, the siren song of a new technology was seductive. Remember, this was the era when computers were really starting to enter popular consciousness. They were appearing on TV shows as a head-shaking novelty. What would they think of next? The media was full of stories of amazing advances and of how industries were reaping huge benefits by using computers.

Now it is true that a lot of companies did benefit from the technique proposed by Dr. S. In the field of diet-blending animal feed it was a total revolution. This technique worked in fields where all the costs, properties, and prices could be accurately determined, and the parts that could be varied were independent of each other. Take feed blending. You have ingredients whose costs keep changing. Each ingredient like oats, lysine, and bran has a nutritional value. Your blend has to meet certain nutritional requirements, e.g. total metabolizable energy must be greater than 2300 calories/kilogram. Various vitamin amounts have to be between certain limits. This is a problem tailor-made for computers. Everything is precisely measured. The costs are exact. The nutritional content of various ingredients comes from recognized laboratories. The software can compute the least-cost blend that meets all of the requirements.

But with software, as we shall see, trying to transfer a solution that works in one situation to a supposedly analogous situation is one of the largest reasons for failure. Yes, you could regard pulp as a particular mix, i.e. a diet, of species. And some timber could be used for higher-priced lumber, but there were various limits. The cost of logging could be estimated for some of the areas, but some were remote and there was only limited data.

We worked hard and reported how our programs said the wood should be harvested, but I noticed that there didn't seem to be any enthusiasm by the people who actually ran the operation to take our advice. I talked to some of them and they told me that our results were not really taking into account some of the practical considerations. We would indicate that a certain area should be logged but they explained that logging that area would require a logging road, and it had to be built through other areas, and it would be necessary to log those areas first to gain access.

We had failed because one criterion for successful implementations of this method was an independence of the various choices, and in this situation the choices were not independent. There were certain areas you couldn't log unless you had logged others before it.

As is usual in application of scientific methods to business, you simplify your problem to make it easier to solve. But you cannot simplify so much that the solutions are just not useful. We were busy pumping out solutions that were, as far as the operational people were concerned, total nonsense.

However, over the years I worked there in the summers and part time during the school year, Dr. S.'s empire grew and absorbed other departments that used computers, such as the data processing operations and accounting.

This is part of a pattern that I observed many times in my career. That is, the length of time between the start of a doomed technology project and when the axe finally falls is mystifyingly long. In the forestry company, it went on for years. Dr. S. was very smooth and covered his losses by absorbing other departments, taking attention from the reason he started there. It's a kind of corporate Ponzi scheme that I've seen practiced a lot. You start a project with grand announcements that you are going to increase profits unbelievably. Then, based on the never-quite-delivered results, you convince upper management to give you more responsibility, so you keep on growing. As you grow you reorganize your new areas to fit your new, modern way of doing things and that, of course, delays having to produce results, and oh—that first thing—it was just a small thing compared to all my new responsibilities, but it is just about to really pay off... This goes on until it ends as all Ponzi schemes do—in a crash.

Black Friday—layoff time.

Out of pure chance I was away and came in the Monday after. They had laid off all the programmers and all the managers, up to and including Dr. S. The whole OR approach was abandoned and the accounting department that Dr. S. had taken over as it computerized was turned over to safe hands, managers who had come from the operational divisions. I never saw Dr. S. again; it was as if he never existed.

However, I had done well—the position had paid my way through university and launched me into a profitable career. The rest of the programmers scattered throughout the community taking jobs at other companies. Over the years I saw this scenario play out time and time again. For example, I encountered the deserted office situation another time. In the 1970s I was working for Computer Science Corporation and went to visit a client, McMillan Bloedel, the largest pulp and paper company in the province. I stepped off the elevator and found that the whole floor was deserted. It had been totally gutted, with ceiling tiles in disarray, cables hanging down, and a scattering of paper and some odd bits of computer equipment dumped on a dirty, dusty floor. A computer department occupying the whole floor of a building had been totally eliminated.

After a while I came to expect it. When recruiting programmers for a project I would look around to see what company or project was being closed down. There was almost always a sudden rush of good applicants because of something being cancelled elsewhere.

Over time I realized it was the nature of the software business, especially enterprise software. So many projects were started with high expectations, went far over time and over budget, and then were canceled, often with accompanying layoffs. Not that any of the programmers really suffered. Good programmers were always in demand and it never took them long to get another job.

Unfortunately, the software business lends itself to a level of hucksterism that causes these booms and busts. It is an easy industry in which to pretend to be knowledgeable and to charge large amounts of money for advice. The customers are often naïve in that they accept the advice without any kind of due diligence. However, to be fair to them, it is very difficult to get an objective, informed opinion, as a large number of supposedly reputable consultants are also posers.

In a lot of ways this is unique to the software industry. Other industries with high technical content, such as medicine, engineering, and architecture, have extensive regulations and certifications. The software industry has none of that. There are some qualifications that people can acquire but none have anything even close to the recognition in legislation for lawyers, doctors, and accountants.

The effect of this is that anyone can claim to be an expert and advise companies on software.[4]

I have started our journey here because it is necessary to point out that, when it comes to enterprise computing, the media is full of information and advice from academics, marketers, and consultants who have never built an enterprise system in their whole career. Most of them don't even know how to program. They have no idea of what really happens in a software project and yet are totally willing to charge for advice about how to run one.

As Yogi Berra said "In theory there is no difference between theory and practice, in practice there is."

There is a cacophony of opinion in the media, and with companies trying to sell their expertise. If you start enquires about ERP[5] systems you will be flooded with content marketers who will send you endless emails telling you what you should do to get a successful ERP implementation.

In this book I'm going to show you what the real issues are, and they aren't what most ERP "experts" will tell you. These "experts" are coming mostly from a theoretical stance,

---

[4] I don't want to sound as if I'm advocating for strict government certification. If there was certification it would probably certify exactly the wrong people. A lot of underperforming experts have considerable academic qualifications as well as recognition from various industry groups.

[5] ERP stands for Enterprise Resource Planning—it means a system that handles most if not all of your operations. It's a terrible name but we seem to be stuck with it.

having never written any software and not knowing what really goes on in these large projects. They stay away from the grungy issues like actual programming. Instead they talk a lot about communication and strategic plans.

This is a lot like discussing the problems of a restaurant without ever looking at the quality of the food.

I receive emails on a constant basis telling me what I should do about my ERP system. I receive them because of the research I have been doing into enterprise system failure. Often to get information you have to surrender your contact info, and the result is a steady stream of emails offering consulting advice, white papers, and a host of other marketing materials that will "help me solve the ERP problems that I surely have."

I recently got one entitled "Four Reasons to Ditch Your ERP Project." The authors warn me that I may be "forging ahead with an ERP implementation without a clear plan or consideration of all possible alternatives."

Then they give four reasons why perhaps I should stop and not do that large ERP system I was thinking of. These reasons are:

- My business process may be the source of my problems.

- My organizational design may be the source of my problems.

- Maybe I should be looking for different software—software that doesn't try to cover the entire organization.

- My first step should be a "technology-agnostic enterprise and digital transformation strategy."

In "advice" like this, they never mention software or programming. It's as if programming is the crazy aunt in the attic who shouldn't be talked about. After all, it's complicated, technical stuff so who wants to talk about that? It is much easier to talk about business processes or having a technology-agnostic digital transformation strategy.

What is a software expert? Can you become a surgical expert without ever having performed a surgical operation? Can you be an expert trial lawyer without ever having defended or prosecuted a case in court? I'm pretty sure most of us would say no—you only become an expert by actually doing the job.

However, in software it seems that there are all kinds of people billing themselves as software experts who have never actually built a system. They aren't really aware of any of the real issues that can decide a system's success or failure. Most of them cannot program a computer.

Yet they are "experts." If you want to know what system to choose, how to implement it, and why it all went wrong, they will gladly charge you lots of money for their advice.

They write articles, books, and give lectures. A lot of them come from large software companies and are trying to sell products. Some are academics who write theoretical papers but have never had practical experience, and some work for consulting companies.

Is their advice worth anything? Should you pay any attention to it? These are questions that we are going to be looking at.

I am bringing this to your attention at this early point in this book because a lot of what I say is totally against all the received wisdom of these experts. If you talk to them, they will say that the problems with enterprise systems are caused by: lack of communication, bad strategy, and/or the users entering everything into the system incorrectly.

It is never the result of a bad code base that was made even worse with bad programming. That is because these experts are not really versed in programming and don't want to get dragged into areas that would show their expertise to be lacking.

Everyone is walking around the elephant in the room—that software is computer code written by programmers.

Don't take my word for it, go to the Internet and search for "enterprise system failure causes."

When I do this I see all kinds of lists: "10 reasons for ERP implementation failures" or, "four common reasons for ERP failure," but when I look through the articles I can't find anybody talking about bad or incompetent programming. The word programming doesn't occur once. It's as if the programmers just don't exist.

This blindness of the consulting community to the actual existence of programming is an example of something that happens when you try to fit a new thing into an old model.

Suppose you are running an aircraft manufacturing company and it buys airplane engines. Then suppose there is a problem with the engine when installing it into the airplane you are constructing. What are the possible problems?

Well, you could have the wrong kind of engine, a mistake in the specifications, or the engine might have a design flaw—maybe it vibrates at high speeds. These are all possible issues and the responsibilities lie with your company, or the supplier, or maybe a split between both. But notice nobody is ever talking about the workers who built that engine. They built what they were told to build and if there is a design flaw, that is the fault of the engineers who designed and tested the engine.

That is the way we view most equipment acquisitions. Any issues are the responsibility of the company that designed and built the equipment.

Enterprises, and the industry around enterprise systems, want to treat enterprise systems as a product; one that is acquired and installed as an airplane manufacturer would acquire and install a jet engine. There is an assumption that the product is totally reliable and will perform to spec, that it has been thoroughly tested and, in a sense, certified by a reputable manufacturer. When you work with this mindset the programming quality is not a factor. Just as one doesn't question the manufacturing quality of a jet engine being designed and produced by a world-class company.

We shall see the problems caused by these kinds of assumptions when we blindly try to carry what works in the physical world into the software world. We will talk much more of this in later chapters, but here I want to point out that this confusion, this disconnect between the reality of enterprise software and of desperately hanging on to old strategies, creates a fertile ground for "experts" of all stripes to extract outrageous amounts of money from enterprises, that then have to live with the consequences.

Over the years I found that there were more and more people in the industry who were pretenders about their knowledge. Computer technology seems ideally suited for all kinds of pretensions—from the minor sin of exaggerating one's resume, through posers trying to pretend that they are knowledgeable, and ending up with fraudsters who use confusion about computer technology as a weapon to confuse and defraud victims.

Enterprise systems are a goldmine for less-than-capable practitioners. There are large amounts of money involved, which is always a necessary condition to attract the less ethical. The business community has less understanding of computer technology than one might imagine. It's almost as if the reaction to the (undeniable) complexity has been to withdraw and not think about it. To make things even better for the poser, there is no real accountability.

Suppose you take someone's advice and buy a certain kind of software, and have it modified to your needs—and it all falls apart. The system is plagued with bugs. All the results are wrong. It crashes constantly during data entry. It is so slow that you fear you will retire before any results are produced. You are in trouble, but what about the consultant?

He or she will probably be glad to charge you for an analysis of what *you* did wrong. If you are suitably enraged at the original consultant you can hire another one to tell you what went wrong. That's okay, because your first consultant is charging your second consultant's previous client for advising *them* on what went wrong in *their* project.

Businesspeople have been cowed by an unending stream of technobabble; complicated-sounding words used when clients wonder about some obvious defect in their system.

I talked to an IT person who worked for a government agency that was trying to modify some enterprise software to fit the agency's needs. There was an identifier that was confusing all the field workers because it used to be a five-digit number, but with the new software, it had an unneeded letter in front. The staff was told that changing this was impossible. When, the government IT people pushed further, the reason they were given was technobabble about the database being in "fourth normal form" and yada, yada, yada... The implication was that if you were smart enough you would clearly see that this change was just not technically feasible.

Of course, it was a perfectly reasonable request, and the technical staff who said it wasn't should be ashamed that their system was built so badly that there was no central facility for modifying identifiers.

No one wants to seem to seem stupid and appear not to know something, especially something that is mission critical to their job. So business people tend to pull back and accept the "expert's" opinion—despite their common sense telling them that this doesn't really sound right.

Consultants and IT practitioners can hide behind this fog of technical knowledge, charge lots of money, and mostly escape any consequences of failure.

That is not to say that all such practitioners lack true expertise, or that their advice is not good—but how do you find them? How do you tell if a project is going off the rails? What do you do about it? Who do you call? Where is your bullshit detector? Let's help you build one.

To do that, we are going to plunge into the world of software and see what is really going on in these systems. A lot of what I'm saying goes against the grain of conventional wisdom. I'm going to be pointing out how large companies can be worse at building software systems than smaller ones. I'm going to be showing how a lot of the commonly-used technology is a major contributor to system failure. And, I'm going to show how all the experts and their pontifications about software failure are missing the elephant in the room.

3

THINGS ARE REALLY BAD
IN ENTERPRISE SOFTWARE

This could be an extremely long chapter but I'm going to keep it short.

Things are really, really bad in enterprise software.

That's pretty much the whole chapter. I could start quoting stats and numbers or showing graphs and charts. I just don't think I have to. You almost certainly know what I'm talking about.

There is no end of articles, surveys and anecdotes in the news talking about enterprise system failure. The Paragon group for example, produces a highly informative report every year detailing the rate of system failure in this area. You can also look at the Chaos report, and the KPMG report, to name a few others. Basically, they say that around 50% of all ERP projects fail.

50% is rounding up, but remember it is hard to measure a fuzzy concept like software project success, and these surveys largely come from self-reported data. There is an obvious bias for project managers to put a positive spin on their reportage. Consequently, the reported numbers are, no doubt, low, and I personally believe that 50% is a significant underestimation.

Further evidence that enterprise system development is in trouble comes from the steady drumbeat of media reports of massive system failures. Bear in mind, these are only the large ones that are notable enough to justify a story. There are almost as many disasters as there are companies.

Then there is my own informal survey. In the last 15 years of talking to people in social settings I have yet to find someone who doesn't have a story of some system disaster.

Finally, for the last five years our company has been talking to companies and asking them about their experiences with systems. In all that time, having talked to hundreds of companies, we have yet to find one that didn't have significant system problems. There was a massive amount of wasted money for systems that never worked. This ranged from a few thousand in small companies to a $100 million write-off by a law firm.

Yet the industry rolls along, making eye-popping profits. Huge, expensive ads are placed in glossy magazines claiming that this software or that application will increase profit, increase efficiency, and in general solve all of the company's problems.

These days people pretty much take it as a given that computer systems will have problems, and it is well understood by everyone that a lot of them end in disaster.

So, I'm going to just cut this chapter short and assume that you are aware that enterprise systems are in trouble and that they fail at an incredibly high rate. If you doubt this I leave it to you to search the web so that you can see the torrent of reports about enterprise system disasters (the ones that people are willing to admit to).

4
SOFTWARE IS DIFFERENT

An object moving quickly comes up to a barrier. Rather than smashing into the barrier, it vanishes and appears on the other side. Science fiction? No, this is reality. It is the tiny world of quantum mechanics.

Our common sense tells us that objects don't pass through walls without resistance. It doesn't happen in our physical macroscopic world. But in the world of the very small, where quantum mechanics reigns, this and other strange effects are standard behavior. And if you think this is just theory, think again. There is an off-the-shelf electronic component called a tunnel diode (current price around $20) that uses that quantum tunneling effect to amplify microwave frequencies.

Here is a world where our common sense fails us. A world where position and velocity are blurred, and two particles can act as one particle independently of how far apart they are.

Applying our common sense in the quantum world will end up with wrong results and a total misunderstanding of what is going on.

The same is true for software, because just like quantum mechanics, software has odd behaviors that lead to misunderstanding and confusion.

The world of software doesn't follow the same rules as the physical world—it is just different.

What is this difference? And how does it affect enterprise systems?

It all comes down to locality and proportionality of effect. The physical world always has effects that are local and proportional to cause—software does not.

I will show you how this low level and somewhat obvious property of software combines with the concept of entropy (disorder) and makes software projects totally different from physical projects.

I am going to show you why the industry has tried to apply the concepts and strategies of the physical world to the software world with disastrous results. Well, disastrous for you, the customer. For the software industry this completely wrong-headed approach, and the adoption of totally wrong technologies, has led not to being hounded into bankruptcy by mobs of angry clients, but to a revenue bonanza where there is no seeming cap on what can be charged.

In a way it's a perfect money-making system. The software industry makes massive profits, so they are happy. Consultants who recommend an ERP system make large kickbacks, so they are happy. The software industry takes out expensive ads in most media outlets, so the media is happy. Bad software requires more hardware than it should, so the hardware manufacturers are happy.

It's an amazing part of the economy where everyone is happy.

Oh, wait—there's you! Well, sorry, but you don't count. You are the user, the person who has to buy the software and try to make it work for your company. Your job is to shut up and write the check.

There is no voice for users. Software manufacturers charge what they want, and if you complain too much they're liable to put the price up again. They have their clients over a barrel. Once you have installed their software there is no going back. Changing a major enterprise system is a massive, expensive, and risky project. No one enters into such a thing lightly, and the software manufacturers take full advantage.

End users have never had a voice because they have never known what to ask for. They don't like all the failures and day-to-day software disasters. But they don't know what else to do. If they say, "surely there must be something better," the IT people come back with, "well what, exactly? What do you want us to do?" And the end user has no answer.

In this book I'm going to give you things to ask for. I'll tell you what to demand and why you should have it. It's about time that you, the end users, started to assert yourselves, and demand the kind of software you are entitled to, given the monies you are spending.

But before you can do that you have to understand what is going on. You have to see these enterprise projects through a different viewing glass. You have to recognize the reality of what is actually happening and reject the self-serving babble-speak of most of the industry.

You have to understand why your common sense fails you with software; why there are so many common misconceptions about software that lead business people like yourself to make the wrong decisions.

You have to understand what makes software different so you can develop a new common sense that doesn't steer you astray and lead to system and business disaster.

Before we start, let us look at some basic information that any person dealing with software systems should have.

5
15-MINUTE EXECUTIVE
BRIEFING ON COMPUTERS

What do you have to know to manage technical issues in areas outside of your own expertise? Managers have been facing this question for as long as there has been management.

All business people deal with a variety of external systems—the banking system, the legal system, and often regulatory systems. We take for granted a lot of the knowledge we need and the terminology we have to understand. To operate with the banking system, a business person has to know about compound interest, overdrafts, lines of credit, loan amortizations, and a lot more. The tax system is incredibly complicated, and even though businesspeople often have tax experts on call they are still required to know about a myriad of issues such as: depreciation, taxable dividends, allowable deductions, payroll taxes, and property tax, to mention a few.

People who don't understand the basic concepts of these systems are routinely defrauded by smart operators. Most business people have a well-defined common sense in these issues. If an investment is offering staggering returns far above any standard investment then the experienced person knows that this is just too good to be true. Naïve people are vulnerable to fraud as they have not developed a sense of how the markets work and what is reasonable and what is not.

All this is knowledge that is necessary for any businessperson to operate in the modern world. How did we get this knowledge? Some was taught in schools but a lot of it is picked up in the day-to-day experience of working in businesses.

When it comes to enterprise computer systems there is a lack of the kind of understanding that business people have with other systems. They understand the basics of the legal, tax, and other systems; they have a feel for them and they can make informed decisions. When it comes to enterprise systems, my observation is that business people do not really have a sense of what is reasonable and what is not. They don't know how the systems work inside, they don't know how they are built, and they don't know what can go wrong with them.

This chapter is intended to bridge that knowledge gap. I present here an executive briefing that will enable us to talk about various issues without a lot of unexplained and confusing terms.

I have structured this as if you are starting at zero, because I have no idea of what you may or may not know. To do this I have decided to follow history. Technologies, as they develop, get more complicated as more and more detailed issues are encountered and solved. When you see the final result, it is quite intimidating—a whole body of knowledge that is presented in its final and polished form. This chapter reviews the beginnings of computers, the time when engineers were trying to figure out how to make something useable. When engineers are exploring new domains, they have to start inventing words, and some of these words pass over into common usage.

TERMINOLOGY

To explore the world of software we need to have a common language and understanding of the basic concepts.

32

Software is not as difficult as it is often presented. There are a lot of people and companies that have an interest in making it seem complicated, even mysterious, and hence expensive.

There is a lot of terminology in software and computer systems, and the industry has no hesitation in swamping you with a torrent of it. I pledge not to do that to you in this book.

One thing to realize is that when these concepts were first invented computer scientists had no words for them. So, as is normal, they made up some and borrowed words for others.

Take the word code. It is used as a noun, as in "computer code," or a verb, "he coded that software." Before computers a code was a body of laws or rules of behavior like a moral code.

Someone decided that software was like a group of laws or rules, so they called it code. And now it is entrenched in the dictionary with the following definition:

Instructions for a computer (as within a piece of software).

This is a very vague definition, but a lot of computer definitions are vague and used by different people in different ways.

MEMORY

We understand what human memory is, but what is computer memory?

Imagine you are running a machine shop. You sit in your office that looks over a noisy shop floor through sound-proof glass. You hire Alan to work on the shop floor. To let Alan know that there is a phone call for him you install a light above the office window, and you have a switch on the wall by the window. When there is a call for Alan you turn on the light.

Now you hire Betty. You install another light. When there is a phone call for Betty you throw the second switch to signal her.

When you hire Colin, you don't have to put in another light. You just signal Colin by turning on both Alan's light and Betty's light.

But when you hire Denise you have to put in another light. However now you can add Denise's light to all the other combinations for Alan, Betty and Colin and cover the next three employees without having to install a light. We can write these combinations with 1 meaning the light is on, and 0 meaning it is off.

So:

001 Alan
010 Betty
011 Colin
100 Denise
101 Edward
110 Francine
111 George

Now suppose you go home one night, and you kill the power to the light system with the master switch. When you come back in the morning you see the phone is off the hook. That annoys you because you are always telling the employees to hang up the phone. The last person who used the phone is the guilty party—who was the last person to use the phone?

Well you look at your light switches and see that they are set to up-down-up or 101. That is the code for the 5th employee, so Edward didn't hang up the phone.

The light switches "remembered" who the last employee to use the phone was.

That is memory. It might not be what you think of when the word memory comes up, but this is computer memory. It is the word that engineers first thought of when trying to name the concept of a group of switches being able to retain their positions. Of course, memory has all kinds of associations in the English language. But don't make the mistake of taking those human-language connotations and thinking of computer memory as somehow possessing some of them. It is nothing like that. It is just a bunch of switches that "remember" when they are up and when they are down. You can think of computer memory as a long line of millions or billions of light switches.

Each of these switches is called a "bit." The genesis of the word is unclear, but it seems to have originated at Bell Labs in the 1940s. A bit is just something that can be in two states: off or on, 0 or 1. Everything in computers is stored as groups of bits.

We see that the combinations double each time you add a switch (aka a bit) because we have all the previous combinations with the new switch at 0, and all the previous combinations with the new switch at 1.

Eight doublings is 256. When we have 255 employees on the shop floor we will need eight switches and light bulbs.[6] Those eight switches can represent a number from 0 to 255. A group of eight light switches was named a "byte." It seems that the idea was to call it a bite as in taking a little bite out of memory, but the spelling was too close to the word "bit," so they changed the spelling to make it byte. Out of interest half a byte (4 bits) is called a nibble—who said computer scientists don't have a sense of humor?

When you see reference to a megabyte, you can think of a million groups of light switches, and when you

[6] Remember that there is the most common case when there is no phone call for anyone. In that case all the lights are off—but it is one of the 256 states, so you can only signal for 255 employees with 8 lights.

see gigabyte you can think of a billion groups of light switches.

Of course, computers don't use light switches, they use high-speed electronic circuits that can flip from 0 to 1 in less than a billionth of a second. But that's just a detail. When we are understanding something all we need is a conceptual model. Thinking of memory as a long line of light switches is perfectly fine, as it is logically consistent with whatever technology is actually being used.

These switches are in groups of 8 (bytes). Each byte is numbered starting at 0. Engineers decided to call that number the "address" or "location" of the byte.

EVERYTHING IS NUMBERS

In computers everything is a number. As we just saw the *only* thing computers can do is flip those light switches in memory. It can move numbers around by flipping switches at the place the number is being moved to, and do arithmetic operations on them, but underneath it all, at the root level, it is just flipping switches.

What is important in a computer is the intent of the number. We know that computers can handle sound data, video data, and text, to name just a few different types of data. They are all stored as numbers, but what the numbers mean is totally different depending on the intent of the data.

If you took a snapshot right now of the memory of your phone or computer it would be a long list of numbers. There is no telling from those numbers what they mean. What they mean depends on the intent behind why they were put into memory.

Suppose there is a number 65 in one of those bytes. What does that mean? It could be sound level at some tiny moment of time in a sound recording. It could be the intensity of the red in a pixel in a high definition image. It could be the letter "A" being represented by a number according to the ASCII text encoding scheme. Or it could be an instruction for the Central Processing Unit (CPU) to obey.

Computers convert everything into numbers, operate on the numbers and convert things back again.

We have physical devices to handle those conversions. Our keyboards convert letters (i.e. keystrokes) into numbers. Our printers do the reverse, they take numbers from memory and look up the right shape of the letter and print it. Sound systems on our computers take strings of numbers and interpret them as sound intensities over a tiny fraction of time. A high definition sound file may have a quarter of a million sound intensities in a second. The sound system takes all those numbers and uses them to produce sound out of a speaker or headphones. They do the reverse with a microphone, converting the sound intensities to numbers.

The video screens of our computers divide the screen into millions of dots (these dots were given the name "pixel") and each dot has a number for red, green and blue. By turning the pixel color intensity to different numbers, a huge variety of colors can be shown.

Everything a computer communicates with is a device that either takes numbers and converts it to some form of display (including sound) or takes some form of input and converts it to numbers.

But all of this pales in comparison to the ability to store computer instructions.

CODE AS NUMBERS

Alan Turing (1912-1954), despite being one of the most brilliant mathematicians of his time and the author of the fundamental mathematics that underpins all of today's computing, was a deeply unhappy man. He poisoned himself after being arrested for being homosexual. A few years ago, the British government formally apologized for his treatment and granted a posthumous pardon. Turing invented the concept of the stored program, a concept that has revolutionized the world.

Alan Turing worked on computers during World War II, famously being involved in the decryption of the German "enigma" code, but it was his mathematical work before the war that was so important. He showed that if a machine could execute a few, very basic operations it could do any calculation possible. He used a hypothetical machine now called a "Turing Machine" that stored and modified its own programming.

Alan Turing had shown that all calculations could be done if you could just do a few simple operations, and those operations could be expressed as numbers.

This means that numbers are not only data, they can be machine instructions. Engineers designed electronic circuitry they called the Central Processing Unit (CPU). The CPU reads numbers from memory and then does the operation associated with that number.

A sequence of numbers in memory can be a whole list of operations to do. What to call these numbers? Engineers reached into the English language and decided that the word "code" was close to what they were trying to describe. They called that group of numbers "code" or "machine code." Code quickly became a verb, "to code" was to produce computer code and a coder was someone who wrote code.

Code was plural or a verb, so it wasn't handy to refer to in the singular. When an engineer had put together a whole group of code to do a particular calculation there needed to be a name to refer to the thing they had created. The word "program" was chosen. They had written a program. Then, of course, someone who wrote a program became a programmer.

Engineers decided that these simple numbered operations the CPU was performing should be called "instructions." Its English meaning is close—you are instructing the computer to do things.

When the CPU picked up an "instruction" and did a particular operation, another word was needed to describe that. They picked "executing" the instruction. Another word they started to use was "run," because a computer is a machine, and, like a car, it "runs." You can see all these words were arbitrary—they could have just as easily said "performing" an instruction rather than "executing."

So sometimes people say "I'm running this program," or "I'm executing the program." That just means the computer has their program in memory and is executing the instructions one by one.

ASSEMBLY PROGRAMMING

Programming in the early days was really tough, in that you had to produce a series of zeros and ones to refer to the instructions you wanted to execute, and the various memory locations (addresses) you wanted things done to.

Engineers soon realized that the computer could take a three letters abbreviation such as ADD or MOV[7], look it up in a list and produce the right binary number for that instruction.

---

[7] The mnemonics for machine instructions have normally been three letters, just because it is short but enough room to give a somewhat informative name to different instructions. Like MOV to move a value from one part of memory to another. Programmers used to joke that there was an HCF (Halt and Catch Fire) instruction. Referencing that joke there was a TV drama "Halt and Catch Fire" about the early days of the IBM PC.

So they wrote a program that would take a list of instructions, written in text, and convert it to the numbers needed by the computer.

Again, they needed a name. What to call this program that translated text into computer code? They called it an "Assembler," I guess because it assembles code in memory. Because this text was in a rigid format which had to be documented so that other people could write programs, they called the collection of instruction words and the rules that governed their use, a "language." Writing those codes to build a program was called "assembly language programming."

Now there was a bit of almost magic that happened here. The first assembler had to be laboriously coded in zeros and ones. But when it was finally working it became much easier to build programs. That made it easier to build assemblers. And that is when software really took off.

It was a virtuous feedback loop—a program to make programming easier, hence making it easier to write programs that made programming even easier, and so on and so on.

After a while no one worked with zeros and ones. It was all programming with text that was converted into machine code. So that text became known as the "source code" because it was the source of the desired end product, which was the machine code. Source code becomes very important because humans can't do much with the zeros and ones in memory. They need the source code that a human wrote to even begin to understand what the program is going to do. This is why software companies guard their source code. It is where their intellectual property lives. If someone with bad intentions gets a copy of it they can use it to make versions of the software that do malicious things. If a competitor gets a copy of it they can figure out any innovative ideas incorporated into the program.

The word "codebase" started to be used to mean all the source code you had in a project. You could say "I backed up the whole codebase."

PROGRAMMING LANGUAGES

Assembly language programming was a huge jump over putting in machine code of zeros and ones, but it was still very laborious. All your logic had to be built from the very simple instructions that were hardwired into the hardware. Computer scientists started building what were called high-level languages. They were called high level because they were more removed from the machine. Assembly languages had an almost one-to-one correspondence between lines in the program and machine instructions. So that meant a lot of lines to get even simple things done.

Engineers, for example, wanted to do calculations that were specified by mathematical formulae. They didn't want to have to bother with the low-level details of doing computations using large numbers of simple instructions. They wanted the computer to be able to handle something like the equations they wrote in their notebooks and technical papers—very much like the formulas you may use in a spreadsheet today.

Thus, FORTRAN was invented. This was the first language I programmed in. It stood for Formula Translation and was designed for engineering and mathematical calculations. But remember, as Alan Turing showed, if you could do a few simple things you could do anything. Fortran[8] has been used to do an amazing variety of data processing, from scientific to accounting.

---

[8] Back in the day computers could only handle upper case letters so it was called FORTRAN—modern versions of this venerable language now use both cases and the name is written as Fortran.

For these high-level languages, they didn't call the program that converted it into machine code an assembler. Instead they took the word "compiler" and started using it to describe that program. So a "programmer" writes "source code" in a "high-level computer language" and then "compiles" that "code" into "machine code" so the computer can "execute" that "code."

Fortran was followed by COBOL (Common Business Oriented Language) which was designed by Commander Grace Hopper of the US Navy and intended for business people to be able to do their own programming[9]. That goal never really worked out, but programmers used it extensively to do enterprise computing.

These days there are hundreds if not thousands of computer languages with more being created every year.

But you don't have to know all of these languages, or even any one of them. You just have to understand that programmers are writing text which is being turned into computer instructions.

SUBROUTINES AND LIBRARIES

Languages made it easier to write programs but programmers found that they were writing things over and over again. Simple routines, such as going through a lot of text and counting the occurrences of a letter. If you have to describe this every time, you have to give

---

[9] To allow business people to design their own systems was Cmdr. Hopper's dream and it has been the "holy grail" of enterprise computing ever since. Over the decades since the 1950s when Cmdr. Grace Hopper invented COBOL, there have been many other attempts to develop software that would open up enterprise computing to the average business person. So far, they have all failed in that primary goal, and have become just another computer language. It is a problem that I have always been fascinated with and have been working on my own attempt at a solution. I believe I have solved it, but that is another book.

instructions to: get the first letter, test it, add 1 to the counter if it is the letter we are looking for, then go to the next letter and repeat the first three steps, then go to the next letter and repeat, and so on until the end of the text.

That's a lot of instructions and you could be doing this operation in all kinds of situations. So, the concept of a subroutine was started. These common bits of code used in a program could be written once and the same code used in all those situations.

This is referred to as "calling" a subroutine. Again, the engineers had to put a name to this new concept.

The world "call" somewhat fits. Perhaps in the sense of a phone call. Calling a subroutine means turning control over to it, having it execute, and then turning control back to your program so it can continue executing.

When the subroutine is finished it "returns" to the caller code, which then continues on. If the purpose was to calculate something it is said to "return a value."

Subroutines are ubiquitous to all computer languages, but they aren't always called "subroutine." All of the following are names that programmers use for subroutines in different languages: method, function, procedure, sub-procedure, routine, subroutine, subprogram.

They all mean the same thing, i.e. a bit of code that other code can "call."

Early on, programmers started to build groups of subroutines to help with specialized tasks. For example, there could be a lot of code to do statistical calculations. There are many common calculations, like calculating various probability distributions, or computing the standard deviation of a list of numbers. If there is code already built to do this it is easier to use that code than to rewrite it. These specialized collections of code became common. They had to think of a word for this that they hadn't already used for a computer concept. They decided on the word "library."

Libraries are bunches of computer code that do a specialized group of useful calculations. These can be included with software so that programmers don't have to write all that code themselves. For example, we have many image formats today: png, jpeg, and tiff to name three common ones. There are libraries that handle reading these formats into some common form in memory. It would be rare for a programmer to actually go to the specifications for those image formats and write all the code to read and decompress the image. They normally include an image handling "library" of code to do this.

A project will also have internal libraries. These are parts of common code in the project that is packaged into a library that is then used by all other parts of the project.

DEBUGGING

What do programmers do all day?

Programmers are either adding to existing code, or trying to find the errors in code, which is called "debugging."

Why is it called debugging? Supposedly Cmdr. Hopper (the inventor of COBOL) was working on a mechanical computer (before electronic computers were developed) and an insect got caught in the contacts, causing the machine to produce an incorrect result. She found the bug and glued it down to her notebook. Since then finding and fixing problems with software has been called "debugging" and the actual flaws are called "bugs."[10]

When computers first started and engineers were entering in simple programs, they found that they couldn't seem to lay out a program without making a mistake.

---

[10] There are references to bugs in machines by engineers in the 1920s, so this story may well be apocryphal.

This was surprising to them, but as careful as they tried to be, these mistakes were always there. The only way to correct them was to run the program and see where it did something differently than expected.

This inability to write computer programs without making mistakes has been a constant in the whole history of computers. To make mistakes when specifying logic is an innate human tendency. We cannot escape our nature; making logic errors is part of our DNA. When it comes to writing software, human beings are incredibly error-prone.

So correcting mistakes is a large part of software development. This is in contrast to physical projects, where issues are worked out in the design phase, and the build and operation of the project can be essentially problem-free.

Most debugging is done by running another program called a "debugger" while your code is executing. This debugger can put stop points into the code you are debugging. It can then show you all the memory locations and their values. You can single step the program to see it operate line by line, until you see it do something unexpected. Of course, the computer is always doing exactly what you told it to do. Unfortunately, we humans are not very good at figuring out all the logical consequences of our instructions, or even setting out the instructions correctly in the first place.

Debugging often requires a special environment, and hence the debugger is often not available when a system is actually running operationally. Computer systems are running billions of instructions a second, so figuring out where something went wrong, without a debugger to help you, can be challenging if not impossible.

Bugs are quite often a simple transposition of symbols, such as typing $<$ (less than) rather than $>$ (greater than). A simple mistake like that can send your software careening off into execution paths you never planned on. There is something about the human mind that tends to transpose things, reverse things, and forget things. So when programmers write software they often make these kinds of mistakes, and consequently cannot avoid lots of time spent in debugging.

When you are writing any kind of software you will have a bug list. This is a list where bugs are recorded when discovered, assigned a number, and have supporting information attached. All programmers have to tackle fixing bugs from such a list. It is very time consuming and removing each bug means being like a detective and solving a crime. Sometimes you catch the bug red-handed. An example might be a bit of text appearing incorrectly in a screen heading. You go to the code that constructs the heading and fix the text. I love those ones. It's a quick fix and I get to take the bug off my list and re-assign it for retesting. Then there are the Agatha Christie-level bugs. These are nefarious, devious hidden bugs. For example, a communications link is shutting down once every few days. You pore through the code looking for clues. It is impossible to put a debugger on it because you never know when it is going to happen, and there are legitimate reasons for the communications to close which happen all the time. You have suspects, but it takes a long while before things become clear, and you see that in certain rare circumstance one part of the code can hit a narrow window of opportunity and do something out of order. Case closed, suspect terminated. That takes a long time and a lot of deduction. That is one of the main things that programmers do all day.

CRASHES

Instructions are stored as numbers, like everything in a computer. The CPU is responsible for taking each instruction number and doing the corresponding operation. But what happens if the number doesn't correspond to an instruction? This is called an "illegal instruction."

In the beginning, the computer just turned on a red light and stopped. There are many ways this can be caused. If a programmer makes an error and directs the computer to start executing instructions at a point in memory that has data rather than code, the computer will just act unpredictably and probably quickly encounter an illegal instruction. The engineers started calling that behavior a "crash." I always thought that was a drastic word for this behavior as it gives non-programmers the impression that it is destructive. It is more like stalling a car by not giving it enough gas, so it just stops. I think "stall" would have been a better word, but we have crash. It is an indication of how taking English words to name new technical phenomena will cause people to apply existing connotations to the word when they don't apply in that situation. Crash has the connotation of damage and disaster, while a computer crash is just the machine stopping because it has reached a situation that it has no procedure for.

If you are running a program on your computer today, and a bug makes it try to execute an illegal instruction, the program will stop and turn control back to the master program, i.e. the operating system.

However, if the operating system encounters such a situation it has no program to turn control back to so you get something like the BSOD (Blue Screen of Death) that happens sometimes on Windows. The computer just displays some technical stuff and stops. You have to restart it with a physical interruption of power to get it going again.

There are all kinds of situations that cause these kinds of behaviors, like trying to divide by zero, or an infinite loop where the program executes the same code repetitively with no way of stopping. In the latter case it may just sit there busily running but ignoring everything else until rebooted.

COMMENTS

In all programming languages, without exception, there is the ability to add notes that are called "comments."

A comment is a statement in the code that is marked as such. For example, in a lot of computer languages a comment would look like:

```
// this is a comment for humans
```

Comments are totally ignored by the computer. They are skipped when the code is executed.

But comments form a large part of the real documentation of the code. Comments explain what the code might be doing. Things like:

```
// the following code is necessary because we
// have to wait for 10 seconds for all the drivers to start
// if you jump in too soon then the system can
// crash intermittently
timeDelay 10
```

This is a typical case for a comment. A programmer has stumbled over a problem. The system crashes on start up once in a while. So, she traces it down to the fact that when the system starts up it takes time for some devices to initialize. If the program tries to use them before they are ready this can cause unexpected results such as a crash.

However, the programmer didn't want to just leave the code with no comment. Some other programmer could be looking at it in the future and think, "Why is it delaying 10 seconds here?" and remove it, thinking it would speed things up, and hence reintroduce the bug.

So the programmer added this comment. It is detailing information that is not readily discernable. This is entirely up to programmers, whether to leave a comment or not. If they are under pressure they tend not to. It is also a judgment by the programmer on what other programmers might know or not know. If they feel that the reason they are doing something in the code is obvious they will see no need to leave a comment. Some programmers just don't write comments under any circumstances.

Sometimes comments are misleading. Someone can write a comment like:

// this subroutine deletes all temporary files

But, after that was written, another programmer changed the code so that the subroutine doesn't delete some of the temporary files. Then a third programmer saw the comment and used the routine thinking it would do what the comment said. After a while the disk fills up with undeleted temporary files causing a crash in some totally unrelated bit of code when it tries to create a new file.

There is a large amount of this knowledge that is kept in programmers' heads—programmers who wrote the software and might understand it completely. Quite often they don't comment all of their knowledge because it is too tedious, and largely impractical. It is very difficult to figure out what to write in a comment and what not to. The result of this is that a lot of project knowledge exists in the heads of programmers, and it's simply not realistic to say, "Write everything down."

NAMING

A large part of computer programming is naming things. Programmers sit in front of their computers and strain to come up with the right names for things.

The computer doesn't care. If you call a subroutine xxs33 there is no problem (for the computer). The computer is going to change the name to a number anyway, so as long as the name is unique it is perfectly okay. The importance of the name is purely for humans to read the code and try to understand what it is doing. So instead of calling it xxs33 a programmer might name it something like returnCountOfBytesNeededToStoreInvoiceList which gives some kind of sense of what that subroutine is going to do. Of course, if some other programmer has changed the subroutine's code then the name may be totally misleading.

Just like comments, some programmers put a lot of care into names, and some just call it the first thing that comes into their heads.

You can name a subroutine to be something informative like searchInternetSitesForAsset.

This gives someone trying to understand the code an idea that this routine will access the internet which will probably take much longer than an in-memory search. If the subroutine is just called searchForAsset someone reading that code may be unaware that this is an expensive operation and call it over and over again. It may not be an issue when the code is being debugged and tested, but in real-life operation, when accessing real websites, it may run very slowly.

So, naming is very important, and an integral part of the human side of programming that I will describe in more detail later.

A FEW OTHER TERMS

ALGORITHM—This is a term that you hear a lot associated with Google. Media articles talk about Google's algorithms.

Algorithm is just a fancy word for "step-by-step procedure." If you can specify how to do a task with a step-by-step procedure then that specification is an algorithm.

Therefore, every computer program is an algorithm. Computer programs are exactly step-by-step procedures. Every line in the program is a step. A computer executes each line in the program one after another unless directed to another line to start executing there.

An algorithm is independent of a particular computer language. A program is just an algorithm implemented using a particular computer language.

ERP—short for Enterprise Resource Planning. This rather meaningless name is applied to systems that cover most, if not all, of an organization's operations. There are no rules as to what makes software something you would call ERP, it's basically a marketing decision. ERP software typically covers accounting, and operations such as time-billing, inventory and customer information. They are normally programs that are customized to fit an organization.

FEATURE—This is a word that is used a lot in software. It just means some capability of the software. Programmers are always adding "features". Perhaps a programmer is asked to provide a button to sort a list on the screen. That is a new feature as it is a capability that did not previously exist. Programmers will joke that some strange behavior is not a bug, but a feature.

SUMMARY

I hope that was useful. I don't want to use a lot of technical terms, but this is a new domain and it has its own dialect.

6
SOFTWARE IS NOT
LOCAL OR PROPORTIONAL (NLP)

Bill was an intern who showed up one day unannounced. He had been sent by HR because Calvin in HR had heard the project team was shorthanded. As it was described to Bill by Calvin, the system the project was maintaining was taking in the company's orders, combining them with previous customer history, and sending them out to various divisions. These orders came from web sites all over the world, and from a large room of telephone operators.

The system had had a rocky start. It crashed continually for the first while but now it seemed to be somewhat stable. What they were dealing with now was a long list of complaints by the users all over the company. The project team was trying to figure out why some of the orders took so long to reach a destination. Some of the reports didn't balance. Needless to say, there was a lot of stress in the team. Management had replaced the project leader, and the new project leader was scrambling to address the problems.

Bill showed up at a bad time. The team had just arrived and they were all whispering about Steve. Steve was one of the senior programmers on the project and he had been under intense stress due to all the problems with the system. Last evening while working his usual sixteen-hour days he had lost it, yelling at the project manager and then hyperventilating and passing out.

After a brief visit to the ER, he had been driven home. His husband had threatened to take a carving knife to anyone who came to their house and talked about work.

No one knew anything about an intern, and the project manager was deep in a meeting about the Steve situation. One of the programmers nodded towards Steve's desk and told Bill to camp out there until he could talk to the project manager. She suggested Bill log into the corporate internal web site and read the technical description of the project.

When Bill sat down at Steve's desk he noticed that Steve had left in the middle of editing a program. He went back and asked the same programmer what he should do. He had to interrupt her and she looked cross. After he explained, she looked at him witheringly and curtly told him to just shut it down and log into his own account.

Bill went and closed the program. However, it said there were uncommitted changes and gave the option of committing them. Bill didn't want to ask the programmer but he didn't want to lose anyone's work. Bill clicked the button that committed Steve's changes to the master code base.

At that moment the project manager showed up. She had been told about Bill being sent down by HR. She rolled her eyes and vowed to herself to talk to HR and ask them what they were doing. HR knew they were having problems, especially with Steve now gone. How on earth could they handle an intern?

She smiled at Bill and said that, unfortunately, they were too busy to really give an intern the work experience he deserved, and sent him back to HR.

Bill's time on the project was about 10 minutes.

Steve had been in charge of all the measurements of system performance. There were a lot of delays in all the system communication and it required constant monitoring. At the time he got into the argument with the project management, he was working on figuring out some of these performance issues and was running test orders on his computer. Steve was trying to catch a problem that seemed to happen when there were a lot of orders all hitting at the same time. He had built a program that would generate a huge number of orders with random timings to try to catch the situation that was causing the bug.

He had a theory that the bug happened when there was a burst of orders happening in a short time. So he put in a test that detected such a burst and then started logging the orders from then on. When there got to be more than 100,000 in the log he didn't want his log files to overflow, so he changed the order number to zero for any orders that came after. He knew that all the software was set up to ignore orders with a zero as an order number. He often used that feature to do some testing when the system was running.

Steve never intended that change to go into the production code, it was just a quick patch to help his testing.[11]

At the moment when Bill had his brief stay on the project they were running version 7. At the end of every month they had a scheduled shutdown to update the software. So, as scheduled, three weeks after Bill left, at midnight everyone logged off and they shut the system down. They started it up with version 8 of the code. Unfortunately, Steve's debugging code was included in this new version.

---

[11] All programmers do this. In my company we referred to these as "medical experiments." All programmers have also experienced a bug where they forgot to delete their medical experiment.

Things were pretty slow for a couple of days and then a burst of orders hit. That started Steve's counter and it took about 10 days to reach a hundred thousand orders. After that, customer orders just disappeared. As it happened, this was in the middle of the night, but they were running a 24-hour operation and the night staff noticed that the orders suddenly dried up. Over the phone the CIO ordered a shutdown and called in all the staff.

People staggered in at 3 a.m. They had no idea of why it had happened. There was no log of anything untoward; the orders were just vanishing.

They started the system up again. All that backlog caused a rush of orders, so the counter started again from zero. To the staff everything seemed fine. Orders were flowing, everyone relaxed. It took about 10 days to reach 100,000 orders, and again the orders started disappearing.

The project team frantically tried to diagnose the problem, but it was difficult. They didn't have a way of running a debugger while the system was operational. When they ran it in a test environment they never got the volume of orders that happened in real life, hence Steve's counting routine never got activated. Consequently, the problem never showed up when they tried running test orders. Steve's test environment that generated bursts of orders might have revealed the problem to be what he had been working on, but it was lost when Steve's machine was wiped and turned over to another developer.

There was another factor that made finding the bug nearly impossible. Computer programs often run many background tasks, just as a clock on your computer desktop keeps running in the background while you are using other programs. Steve's monitoring software was running as a background task, and when it changed the invoice number it was doing it at random timings, so it could happen at any stage of processing the order. When the frantic programmers tried to figure out what was causing the problem there was no logic to the stage at which things were happening.

They shut the system down and started it up again. Of course, now it worked with no problem because the counter had been reset.

By now the project team realized that the system failed after it had been up a certain time. They started to bring it down and restart it every week. This worked until their business grew, and it started happening every four days, then every three. After a while they had to stop and restart the software every day. This meant that the telephone room had to shut down an hour every day and miss all those orders, and the websites had to be changed to accumulate orders when the main system was down. This took a lot of programming and testing.

The irony is that, as part of some other maintenance work, parts of the monitoring system were rewritten, and Steve's code with the debugging change was unknowingly replaced. So now the system would run indefinitely but no one knew that. Every night they took the system down and restarted it, despite that being a massive amount of work which required hiring an extra six staff.

They were afraid to let it run longer than a day because previously it had always started to drop the orders.

So that simple, mistaken click on a button by Bill, an intern who was only working on the project for 10 minutes, caused a massive problem that went on for months, resulted in the loss of business, took all the resources of the programming department to investigate, necessitated the hiring of additional staff, and forced the company to continue to operate in an inconvenient and inefficient fashion.

A tiny action caused a staggering problem. This is an illustration of a fundamental property of software—NLP.

NLP

Non Locality and Proportionality (NLP): In software, an effect is not proportional to the cause in either locality or severity.

This is a key principle of software, a principle that is so obvious (once you know about it) and so subtly powerful.

In software nothing is proportional, nothing is distant, and nothing is small. In the software universe everything is connected. A single bit changed in one remote part of a software system has the potential of causing almost any effect, anywhere else in the software.

This simple observation is at the base of all our problems with Enterprise software.

Right now, you may be thinking "Really? That's it?" Stay with me here. I'll show you how this principle impacts the way we write software, the way we try to control software projects, and the way we regard software failure. Just because a principle is simple doesn't mean it cannot have far-reaching and incredibly complex results. For example, consider the simple principle of "survival of the fittest," and the complex biodiversity that has resulted from it.

NLP AT WORK

On June 4, 1996 an unmanned Ariane 5 rocket launched by the European Space Agency exploded just 40 seconds after its lift-off from Kourou, French Guiana. The rocket was on its first voyage, after a decade of development costing $7 billion. The destroyed rocket and its cargo were valued at $500 million. A board of inquiry investigated the causes of the explosion and in two weeks issued a report. It turned out that the cause of the failure was a software error in the inertial guidance system. It was a one-word mistake. Buried in millions of lines of code was a single word: INTEGER should have been DOUBLE.

This seemingly simple mistake caused the destruct system to misinterpret the horizontal velocity. It was expecting the velocity to be in units of kilometers per hour, but a change to the system measuring the velocity meant it was being measured in tiny units of a fraction of a meter per second. So instead of the small number the destruct system was expecting it got a huge number. The destruct system interpreted that large number as a massive negative horizontal velocity—which meant the rocket was heading back to the launch area at an incredible speed. It had no choice under that interpretation other than to destroy the rocket.

A tiny error but a massive consequence—this is NLP at work.

This is not the only expensive space mission to be destroyed by a software error. In 1962 the Mariner 1 spacecraft lost control because of a single wrong character in a data set, and it had to be destroyed to avoid it crashing into an inhabited area. That mission represented a sizeable fraction of NASA's budget at the time.

COMMON SENSE AND PHYSICAL SYSTEMS

Common sense is defined as "good sense and sound judgment in practical matters." Common sense is a set of expectations of common situations. We developed this common sense right from the start of our lives as babies looking curiously from a crib at sunlight shifting in the room, and from play as we stacked blocks and watched them tumble down, and from eating as we poured water from a jug to a glass and saw how liquids flow. Our whole life is a constant reinforcement and application of our common sense.

This common sense serves us through school and into our chosen careers. It is part of us and, as we shall see, it impacts all of our decisions.

Common sense is so omnipresent that most of us just accept it. We don't try to analyze it—it just is. We grew up with it and incorporated it into our very being. It is so much part of us that we never really question any of it. This is why things like software, things that don't obey the physical rules that our common sense is based on, can be so frustratingly difficult to deal with.

One of the things we absorb as a natural feature of the world is a Locality and Proportionality Principle.

Locality and Proportionality Principle (LP): In the physical world an effect is proportional to the cause in both locality and severity.

This is the reverse of the NLP principle of software. The physical world is proportional and has locality, software is not proportional and has no locality.

The proportionality of the physical world is so fundamental that you have probably never really thought about it—but it dictates how you manage projects, how you manage people, and your whole view of how things work and how processes can be improved.

In the physical world everything is local and proportional. Effects can travel, of course, but they always weaken over distance.

Managers responsible for software projects have always looked enviously at projects such as bridge building. These kinds of projects look as if they are far easier to control. Sure, there are budget and schedule overruns, but nothing like the chaos and unpredictability that rules in the software world.

Bridges are built with incredible safety factors. Engineers calculate the maximum load—for example, suppose a bridge of given weight (static load) is packed with cement trucks (dynamic load), and there is a dump of wet snow over the entire bridge (snow load), and on top of that the wind is blowing hard (wind load). They take the sum of those loads to derive a maximum, and make sure the bridge will stay up even if the actual load is some multiple of that totally unrealistic maximum. This ensures that the bridge is built to tolerances far, far beyond what would normally be expected in every-day usage.

Now suppose that when a bridge girder was installed, a rivet was missed. Missing a rivet is not really a problem. There is so much safety margin that it couldn't possibly threaten the safety of the bridge. But suppose we missed a whole bunch of rivets. When enough rivets are missing there will be a noticeable impact. The bridge at that point may flex, or even slump.

Notice though that the flexing or slumping will occur where the rivets are missing. When the slumping is noticed, maintenance people will instinctively check the supports that are managing to hold the load and discover the missing rivets. It is just common sense that the cause is located close to where they are seeing the effect, i.e. the slumping.

This is a proportionality of effect and location from the cause. The effect is close to the cause and its impact is proportional to the cause. This proportionality is true of physical systems. We learn this as children when we are building with toy blocks. If a building collapses we go right to that point to find out what we did wrong. Maybe we balanced a whole load of blocks on top of a narrow one and as we added to the top it became more and more unstable until it toppled. Notice that the effect is right there. It was all to do with the bottom block; it has nothing to do with another set of blocks your sibling is playing with in a different room.

Imagine on our bridge there is a patch of a girder, maybe on the reverse side that is not visible, that is not painted. That would be largely inconsequential. Over time there may be a rust problem that, if left unattended, could start to become a real problem. But that takes a long, long time, and for a small patch of girder that is not painted but sheltered from the weather, it will never be an issue. You certainly would not expect that missing a patch of paint would cause the other end of the bridge, a kilometer away, to vaporize.

The severity of the effect of that defect is proportional to the defect. A missing patch of paint is such a small defect that it has a correspondingly small impact, and that impact lessens the further away from the cause you go.

SOFTWARE

This is not true of software. There is no proportionality.

Look at the example of Bill the intern at the beginning of this chapter. Just that one button push and some weeks later the entire company is thrown into a confusion that lasts for months and is forced to operate in highly inconvenient and inefficient ways.

In software just because the defect is minor, it doesn't mean that the consequences will be minor. These consequences can be anything from a minor overlap of text in a report, to crashing the system randomly, or to corrupting stored data so that special programs have to be written to bring it back into a consistent and usable state, or to totally wiping out all the data and every backup for the last six months, or anything else that you can imagine.

This is because there is no proportionality in software. In our current, standard computer architecture, the memory of the computer is a shared resource and it is accessible by all parts of the program, so all parts of the program are interconnected.

And now that our computers are connected via the Internet, these non-proportional effects can spread across the world.

Software engineers have always tried to disconnect parts of the software; this is the impetus for Object-Oriented programming which you may have heard mentioned in connection to software. It is an attempt to "encapsulate" bits of software so their internal workings and storage is not as accessible to other software, and hence to reduce interaction. This, and other techniques, have helped in a small way to reduce the non-locality of software. However, it is amazing how pure logic, like software, can find ways to impact something that it would seem to be totally isolated from. The fact is that there is no real isolation in software.

One task on your computer may be running and should not be able to impact another. But, of course, they do. Just by using up disk, or consuming excessive CPU cycles they impact other tasks. There are all kinds of bugs in the operating system that allow one process to interfere with another.

This is unlike physical systems where interconnections are physical in nature and different parts are only remotely connected through a series of physical objects. The patch of unpainted metal is related to the girder it is on, which connects to the bridge deck, which has sections, each one connected to the previous, which eventually gets us a kilometer down the bridge. Any force that is going to be applied to that part of the bridge which is a kilometer away will have to be transmitted down the bridge or through the air/water around the bridge. In physical systems, forces always decrease when they travel. They are proportional to the distance away from the cause, and hence if the end of the bridge is to collapse there has to be a far greater force that originates at the site of the cause. In other words, a major force event like a collapse that occurs remotely from a cause has to be caused by a much, much stronger force event at the source.

SOFTWARE V PHYSICAL WORLD

Suppose you are in charge of a tunneling project. Your workers are using tunnel-boring machines and are boring a long tunnel. They are working from both ends so they can meet in the middle. You have hit some difficult rock and it has slowed you down. You need to make a deadline, so you look for ways to speed up the work. Now suppose the ground above where the middle of the tunnel will be is available to you and you can dig down and put in two more boring machines to speed up the work.

If this all turns out to be cost effective it's clearly a valid strategy. Having four machines instead of two will double the amount of tunnel bored each day and reduce the total time to complete the project.

Notice some assumptions we have made here. We assume that there is no trouble getting extra machines and crews to work them. Tunnel-boring machines are a commodity that can be purchased from large construction equipment manufacturers. There are many people around the world that have experience in this kind of construction work, and if you offer good pay and bonuses there should be no trouble in assembling two more crews to operate the new machines.

So, there is no question here that it is possible to assemble a crew competent to do the job. And if a worker on one of your crews becomes sick, you can hire a replacement.

Another assumption is that there is no impact on the existing crews by starting the new borers. They are several kilometers away and keep on working independently of what the new crews are doing. The only impact on them will be that they will join up with a boring machine coming the other direction much sooner than if the project had remained with only two boring machines.

We are relying here on the locality and proportionality (LP) of physical systems. They are proportional in location and effect. All the four crews are separated from each other by kilometers of rock. Not until they meet up will any event with one crew impact any other.

Notice that the people involved are not really important. Certainly, some crews are better than others and may achieve better results, but that is marginal. It is easy to measure the number of meters per day each team is completing, and if one is significantly slower than the others we can examine that team in isolation to determine the problem and what to do about it.

This approach won't work for software. There is no real independence of different parts of a system and there are not repeatable parts that can be duplicated by different teams. If something is repeatable in software then it is a subroutine, or a function, and would only need to be written once and then used by everyone that needed that functionality.

As Brooks noted in his book *The Mythical Man-Month*, adding more people to a software project will slow it down rather than speed it up. This is in total contrast to our tunneling project, where it was clear that extra crews could speed up the tunneling.

This is the physical world strategy of breaking a project into smaller, more manageable pieces. In our tunnel example we halved the distance each of the original two crews had to tunnel. If the geography and finances allowed it, we could put in even more machines and crews to further speed up the work. It's clear to our physical-world common sense that eight crews would bore tunnel twice as fast as four.

Because of physical system locality, when you break a task into smaller units those units have smaller impacts on smaller parts of the project. If tiny parts are ignored, that neglect will have tiny impacts. Our common sense understands this implicitly.

This guides all aspects of how we run businesses. "Don't sweat the small stuff", "Focus on the big picture", "Don't be a micro-manager".

This has been the management mantra for the whole industrial revolution, and no doubt for all of human history. Why? Because it works!

Physical projects can be divided into small chunks. Things can be separate. "Don't smoke in the gunpowder room" implies a locality of cause and effect. You can smoke outside the gunpowder room—well, preferably well outside—but we instinctively understand that if we separate two situations to two different locations, they will not interact.

Software projects act nothing like this. You shall see that, because of NLP, they act in a totally different manner, and have to be managed totally differently. None of the ways we approach physical systems work with software because of NLP.

NLP is an interesting property, but the real problems begin to multiply when it is combined with "entropy." As we will see in the next chapter, this toxic blend is the major cause of software disasters.

7
ENTROPY

Entropy is a word for disorder, confusion and, at its extremes, chaos. The concept of entropy started in the field of thermodynamics, a rigorous branch of physics, but over time it became clear that it was a more universal concept. Claude Shannon extended it to information theory, where it is used to measure the randomness of data and the strength of cryptography algorithms. In software it is used to conceptualize the confusion and disorder in software under the phrase "software entropy."

Programmers have a concept called "technical debt," which is when a software project accepts a level of confusion and disorder in the interests of getting something completed faster. It is a debt, because that measure of disorder will impede future enhancements and cause future bugs. To fix this it is usually necessary to rewrite those disordered parts of the code to stop them from being a continual source of problems.

All of this is entropy—disorder. Treating it as a measurable value makes it easier to talk about, but although it has a precise scientific definition when applied to thermodynamics or to information theory, when applied to software it becomes a fuzzier concept, as there is no real way of assigning quantitative values.

Consider our example of Bill the intern clicking once on a screen and causing devastating problems. What caused all that? Who was at fault?

Well there were several things that all had to line up. Steve had to leave his computer logged in and in the middle of doing a test experiment. Steve never did that normally. He was a senior programmer and, because of his job handling all the measurements, he had total access to all parts of the source code and all rights to make changes. He was always very careful about making sure he shut down each night.

However, the stress of the project caused some chaos and his machine was left logged in. In all the confusion, Bill the intern was placed at that desk. If a member of the project team had sat at Steve's computer they would have done a compare to see how Steve's code differed from the main branch. It would be clear that it was just debugging code and the programmer would have deleted the test code and logged off.

Bill had no idea of any of this and just thought he was saving something before closing, as if it was just a word processing document. Because he was logged in as Steve his button push had full authority to change the main code base.

Steve should have isolated his test more but he was in a hurry and doing it the quick and dirty way that had always worked for him before.

If Steve had still been on the project he would probably have figured the problem out quickly. He would have remembered his testing and quickly checked to see if he had mistakenly pushed some test code into the main branch.

But all that project knowledge left with him. His familiarity with the measurement code wasn't something you could document, it was human knowledge, which is hard to pass on.

All of these happenings are disorder in the project: the stress causing Steve's breakdown, which led to all his normal procedures being forgotten, Bill being pushed into the project, Bill sitting at Steve's desk with a half-done experiment open on Steve's computer.

You might say, "Well that required everything to line up—what are the chances?" You could instead think of all the billions and billions of possible things that *didn't* happen because factors didn't line up. This was just the one that did. If you have a lot of entropy in a system, there are a lot more ways for things to line up to create a problem, and because of NLP the consequences of those problems are of any scale.

Entropy combines with entropy. Suppose in the example of Bill the intern, the code base had lots of bugs and was always doing strange things. That is high-entropy code, and of course trying to track down why orders were vanishing would become exponentially harder. All the symptoms that might lead to a cause are obscured by the noise of all those unrelated incidents.

If you have a high-pressure project it means that there are frequent occurrences of these kinds of incidents. Most of the time nothing untoward will happen. But it's like continually rolling a pair of thousand-sided dice; if you roll them enough times eventually they will come up snake eyes. When the entropy in a software system increases, the number of possible unfortunate combinations of events grows exponentially. If there is enough entropy in the system the probability that one unfortunate combination will occur approaches 100%.

ENTROPY AND NLP

Entropy is the destroyer of software systems because it combines with NLP. This mix is extremely toxic to software systems. Of course, there is entropy in the physical world. We see disorder in physical systems all the time. Messy supply rooms, badly-maintained equipment, leaky buildings, and all the other things that can be disordered in a physical project. But at least in the physical world there is proportionality to effect. The problem in one physical location will not impact another, and a small problem will almost certainly have small consequences.

Entropy in software is additive because of NLP. That means that entropy combines with other entropy regardless of location and produces small errors that can have disastrous effects.

In the physical world, physical separation is often used for safety. Keep the flammable liquids away from sources of flames. In software this doesn't work. A small spark from one part of the software can trigger a giant explosion in another.

IMAGES OF ENTROPY

Entropy is a quantity that is hard to define precisely but it is nevertheless very real in software projects.

An image for entropy is the trickster, a malignant and malicious entity who is always trying to fool you and cause problems in your project.

When I am working on a software system I am fully aware that I am in a titanic struggle with entropy—the trickster trying to break loose to spread disorder and chaos. You have to always be on your guard when writing software so that you don't let the trickster seize control and send your software into a death spiral with an ever-increasing number of bugs and unpredictable behavior. You have to write clear and informative comments. You have to name things carefully so you will know what they stand for when you look at the code later. You have to put checks in your code to test conditions you believe to be true. You have to put in instrumentation that logs all significant events and can be directed to do even more detailed logging of problem areas. If you ignore the trickster you will pay for it with a series of bewildering errors that are mind-bogglingly difficult to diagnose and fix.

Another image of entropy is that of an ocean current, which is always flowing and will sweep you away unless you expend effort to swim against it.

This inevitability of entropy is known in software engineering literature as Lehman's Law of Increasing Complexity.

"As an evolving program is continually changed, its complexity, reflecting deteriorating structure, increases unless work is done to maintain or reduce it."

In dry academic tones that is a good statement, but to the real-life programmer who has to get the software together and working, it's a lot more personal. It is a constant, wearing battle that you cannot take your eyes off of for an instant, because if you do... The Phoenix system (described earlier), as we shall see when we look deeper, is a demonstration of what can happen when you take your eyes off entropy.

The image I like best is that of a corrosive substance that causes problems in everything it touches. Entropy is auto-catalytic in that the presence of entropy causes more entropy. This is like rust, which expands its area and destroys protective coatings, making more and more of the material subject to it. The reason I like this image is because it indicates how entropy can spread outside of a system into an organization.

When you get a high-entropy software system you are transferring entropy into your organization. That confusion and disorder will spread to different parts. Wrong reports will cause wrong decisions. System errors will cause stress that carries on to other parts of the organization.

When software manufacturers cause issues in your business system because of their own marketing agendas, they are dumping a load of corrosive entropy into your organization. This will negatively impact your outcomes.

PHYSICAL ENTROPY V SOFTWARE PROJECT ENTROPY

Entropy affects all systems, both physical and software. It is just that, because of the NLP property of software, it is far worse in software than in physical systems.

We are used to entropy in physical systems. Any physical project has a degree of disorder. There may be a supply shed where things have been thrown into a big heap on the floor instead of being neatly stored so they can be found easily. There may be a spill on a floor, or tools left around carelessly. Disorder may extend to the building plans, where pages are smudged and hard to read, leading to errors in the build that have to be corrected. All of these issues contribute to the total entropy of the project.

The more entropy there is, the more errors or even accidents are likely to happen. Suppose you go into an automotive repair shop and it is disorganized. Tools are scattered everywhere, there are oil spills on the floor, all kinds of parts and bits of cars are pile haphazardly around the room, and no one seems to know the status of your repairs. That tells you that this is a badly run place. It makes you wonder if you should change to another repair shop to get your work done. We recognize instinctively that that kind of disorder leads to accidents and substandard work. If the repair shop is spotlessly clean, if all the tools have a labeled storage spot, and the mechanics are wearing clean uniforms we sense immediately that this is a well-run shop and probably will produce good results.

We know from our physical world common sense that the messy repair shop is going to be slower to get things completed. The time the mechanics spend searching for the right tool alone will add to repair time. Those oil spills are accidents waiting to happen. Eventually someone is going to slip on one and come down hard on the concrete floor.

So that is entropy in the physical world, but what does it look like in software?

ENTROPY IN THE SOURCE CODE

In the story of Bill the intern, most of the entropy was project entropy.

The code base of a large system like the Phoenix payroll system probably runs over a million lines of code (we shall see that one aspect of high-entropy systems is bloat in the source code). Smaller, more specialized systems would have tens of thousands of lines.

That's a lot of text. There are around 30 lines to a page in a book. So 30,000 lines of code is 1,000 pages which is two really hefty 500-page books. If you have a million lines of code it is equivalent to around 60 books of code. If it takes an average of 500 lines per file, that means a million-line code base will have some 20,000 files. The slightest mistake in any one of those lines can cause the whole system to produce faulty output. Remember our example with Bill the intern—that was just one added line of code and it caused havoc for months.

So, what does disorder look like in source code? It is any kind of error that you can think of, including but not limited to:

JUST WRONG CODE—humans often enter in the reverse of what they mean, or just don't figure out the code so that it works in all cases. As we have mentioned before, humans always create errors when constructing logic. If the programmers are not very good, under stress, or unfamiliar with the project, this will greatly increase the number of errors and drive the system towards instability.

BAD NAMING—if subroutines are named badly it confuses other programmers about the intent of that code and may cause them to call the wrong one.

BAD COMMENTS—comments are annotations to the code that are used by programmers to figure out what the code does. If the comments are badly written or misleading, this can cause a programmer to make wrong decisions and cause more errors.

MIXED UP FILE VERSIONS—there are typically thousands of text files in the code base, plus any number of files with images, fonts, and configurations. With these many files, and a large number of programmers working on them, mistakes are inevitable. Old files with old bugs can be reintroduced into the code base. If the file-naming conventions and directory structure are confusing then errors will inevitably result. Most projects now use a source control system to manage the problem of many people working on the same files, but they are certainly not immune to human error.

UNHANDLED ERROR CONDITIONS—it is hard work to figure out all of the possible errors and what to do with them. If the system doesn't have a robust error-handling standard and strategy, then programmers just start making up ways of handling errors, and there is no consistency. Some programmers ignore them, especially if they are under pressure. So, programs can encounter an error but just keep on working and creating problems further on whose cause is then very difficult to discern.

CUMBERSOME INTERFACES—all systems use libraries to do standard tasks. However sometimes the interfaces to these libraries are clumsy and not well suited to what the system is doing. Chapter 16 shows that relational databases are one of the worst culprits. This kind of library requires programmers to write lots of interface code to translate the needs of the project into the calls and data required by the library. This can spike entropy and start a project off in an already high-entropy state. This greatly increases the problems caused by the inevitable entropy introduced by programming.

All of this is entropy, and if the source code of a software project is full of these kinds of problems it is high entropy. There will be a very high probability that these issues will combine in ways to produce errors, and because of NLP the effects of those errors can be dramatic.

PROJECT ENTROPY

As we have seen, entropy can be disorder in the source code, but it can also be disorder in the project as a whole. The story of Bill the intern showed how putting programmers under stress created a situation where test code was accidentally put into the production system. This disorder in the people system, combined with disorder in the code, illustrates that in software, entropy is not just confined to the code base. This is a feature that will be examined in detail in a coming chapter.

However, to be able to examine this we first need to look at how people have tried over the years to tame the wild perturbations and massive overruns of software projects. This is the topic of software methodologies, a six-decade refusal to accept that software projects are not like physical projects that still continues unabated today.

8
SOFTWARE METHODOLOGIES

While I was writing this book, I watched from my office window as a construction team built a house next to ours. They tore down the old, dilapidated bungalow that had belonged to an elderly lady who had lived there for most of her life. Then they brought in a backhoe, dug a large hole, poured foundations, and proceeded to construct a large, two-story duplex.

Every so often I saw the workers gathered around the blueprints having a conference, with a lot of talking and pointing at some part of the construction. They were, no doubt, deciding what the blueprints specified and how to build it exactly that way.

The one thing they were not talking about is changing the blueprint, i.e. changing the design of the house. It took two years to get those plans approved by the city. Each stage of construction is inspected by a city inspector. If you make an unapproved change the city will red-tag your job, charge you penalties, and force you to go through another time-consuming, bureaucratic process to get the modified plans approved. If your modifications violate the building code they will compel you to rip out your modifications and build something that conforms to code.

That blueprint is sacred. What it specifies is what gets built.

The blueprint is a model for the house being built. This model is on paper, but you could build a scale model from it. If several contractors were given identical blueprints they would all build the same house. The plans specify the lumber to be used, the shape of the roof and even paint colors. Although built by different contractors these houses would be like identical siblings, difficult to tell apart.

We are used to the ability to model things in the physical world. We are used to being able to write specifications that describe the physical thing exactly. We can easily conceive of a robot being able to read a blueprint and build a house. In fact, a lot of blueprints are produced on 3D design software like AutoCAD, so automatic processing of the design is already happening. Model builders use the blueprints to build scale models so that people can see how something looks in three dimensions. With today's augmented reality and virtual reality technologies, that blueprint can be read by software and a virtual model of the house created. This is a neat use of technology, but it seems like a very logical and predictable extension to building scale models out of cardboard and glue.

Scale models, blueprints, and plans are a ubiquitous part of our concept of building things. We just take them for granted.

But software is different, and right from the early days of building enterprise software systems things didn't go as planned. Managers at companies introducing computers into their operations were baffled at how unmanageable software projects proved to be. These projects were running incredibly late, and far, far over budget. The only difference in those early days was the lack of the current resignation and defeatism that exists today. Management at that time was still sure that if they tried hard enough the software management difficulties would be brought under control. After all, this was their experience with every other difficult problem that they had faced in the past. Today, management has had an additional five decades of brutal software experience and is certainly much warier about taking on a large software project.

But not much has changed. People are still trying to fit software into the physical world paradigm, despite all the indications that it doesn't work.

METHODOLOGIES

So how did management and software professionals back then react? They all decided that it must be the way they were doing software. In other words, they just didn't have the right methodology. Surely it was just a matter of organizing things and dividing the project into more bite-sized chunks, just as you would do with a physical system.

They were (naturally) following their physical world common sense—all projects could be conquered if they just used the right approach.

To figure out an approach they turned to the concept of a "methodology." At the time the feeling was—if engineers can build their projects on time and within budget why can't these software people?

Clearly (so they thought) it was because they weren't controlling the projects properly. So, the concept of "methodology" was born. There must be a way to systematically collect all the requirements of a system and proceed to the installation and acceptance of a working system. After all, every engineering problem that had been encountered in the physical world had been solved this way.

In the physical world you design something and then you build it. It was taken for granted that a methodology would have a design phase followed by a build. From the very start there has been an attempt at establishing the status divide of the physical world—that of the designer/architect to the builder. Designers were called systems analysts and the people actually writing code were called coders. It was assumed that after all the difficult issues had been resolved in the design phase, the build would be essentially a mechanical task carried out by those coders.

This model persisted for a while, but as the 1960s rolled by, and then the 1970s, and there was still no sign of improvement, it was starting to become clear that the programming job was far more complicated and difficult than just a robotic implementation of a design. It's not that this concept went away; it still exists today in some people's minds.

I was always both a designer and a programmer because I felt that if you didn't work on the actual code you didn't really understand what was going on, and I liked to understand all the low-level details.

But I wasn't immune from the lure of a methodology. I was ashamed of my always-wrong estimates. I just couldn't seem to get it right. Things always took far longer than I could possibly have believed they would— even after putting in contingency after contingency and adding some padding on top of that.

Back in the 1970s and 1980s, I too believed that I could improve estimates by using the right methodology. Academic papers and articles in magazines proposed the latest methodologies that were "guaranteed" to bring your project in on time and on budget.

And I fell for it. I might be a good programmer, but I couldn't seem to bring a project in on time. Everything seemed to spin out of control, and every project was only finished with a death march to the finish line. Even then, "finish line" was a somewhat blurry concept, because some features were left out entirely, and some features, such as reports which would not be required until the first month end, were still to be implemented. If you're the kind of person who likes to deliver something that works, and works properly, this is painful. All of my systems straightened out over time, albeit a longer time that I would ever have dreamed, but they did finally become totally adjusted to the companies they served. As I moved on to the next project, I always felt that if I had just done things better I could have gotten it done sooner, or at least been able to better predict the schedule and required resources.

In order to achieve that I started to try the new methodologies that were available. With each new project I undertook, I tried whatever methodology was the latest rage. This included: Yourdon, UML, Booch, Spiral, DeMarco, Chief Programmer Team, Prototyping, and others that I can't even remember now.

None of them changed the outcomes. Projects were still difficult, and project deadlines were still continually missed. Each time I was convinced that the methodology I was using was the answer, and yet it wasn't. I ended up thinking that maybe it was me; maybe I was just crap at this software project stuff.

I would have sunk into total despair if it hadn't had been for the fact that all the really good programmers I knew were having similar problems. For a while I was part of a group of programmers from different companies who had a monthly lunch at a Greek restaurant. As we swapped notes and war stories, we realized that none of us was performing any better than anyone else in the group. In fact, given that we were some of the best programmers in town, we were getting better results than programmers on other projects we had knowledge of. At least our systems worked and were used, even if they were late and over budget.

After two decades of trying I gave up. The methodologies all started to sound the same. Basically, they all prescribed breaking the project up into smaller bits, assigning these bits to different programmers, and then getting and measuring estimates for each programmer.

It seems like so much common sense. After all, this approach had been fantastically successful in managing physical world projects, and software projects must be just the same.

In the 1990s I was an owner/partner of a fifty-five-person contract software house, called Paradigm Development Corporation, which provided software contracting services to large software manufacturers like Microsoft, Adobe, and Disney. This gave me a good look into the world of packaged software at the highest level and allowed me to compare this kind of software to enterprise software. I designed and managed our internal enterprise systems which provided me with a continual day-to-day comparison between packaged software and enterprise software.

After we sold our company in 1998, I started to investigate enterprise systems. I was certain they could be done better, and I researched how enterprise systems were built, and how techniques that were developed in the pre-computer past have relevance.[12]

During that research, I started to understand what was happening and why I had been so frustrated for so many years. More importantly (at least to my sense of self-worth) I started to understand why the problems weren't my fault, but were inherent in the situation.

---

[12] The only reality in software is working software, so to research Enterprise systems I had to develop software, called Formever, that implemented my ideas and demonstrated that the objectives were possible.

So now I can lay out for you what is going on and why I, and pretty much everyone else who has ever run a serious software project, cannot seem to bridle the project and bring it under control.

PHYSICAL PROJECTS SPLIT DESIGN AND BUILD

At first people tried to treat these projects with familiar models imported from the physical world. In that approach there was clear distinction between the designer/architect and the builder. In this new software world, architects/designers were called systems analysts, and the builders were called coders. There was an assumption that the roles would be the same; that there would be highly skilled workers who would be the designers and the coding would be left to less-skilled workers who could do the mechanical job of actually writing computer code.

But after a while it became clear that this didn't work. No matter what methodologies were adopted, or how carefully designs were made, it all seemed to come unglued at the coding stage. Things happened during programming that turned the design upside down and rendered the documents useless.

This is the total opposite of physical construction. In that environment the blueprint rules. If you meet a problem where the blueprint is somehow impossible to follow you modify the design and put the modified design through the approval/checking system.

Suppose you have a construction company building a road. They are following the plans they have been given to the fraction of an inch. Now suppose they find an unexpected underground stream that requires that a whole culvert be built below the road, which is not in the plan.

The engineers designing this road would redo the plans for that section of the road, with the culvert exactly specified as to the diameter of the pipe, its length, and maybe even a product number from a supplier. The plan will tell the construction company exactly how deep to set the culvert and every other detail.

You can see in physical systems there is always this concept of the plan—the blueprint. It is the driver of the project. If the design has to change, the procedure is always to update the blueprint and then give it back to the construction crew for implementation.

Notice, too, that the difficulty with this part of the road wouldn't stop work on other sections. In physical construction there is an independence of components.

This is what people tried to do with software systems. It seemed like common sense—how can you argue with doing a design first? "Fix it in the design phase," was always bandied about. After all, it's just common sense that it is more expensive to fix something during the build—certainly that's true in physical systems. In our road example above it would have been much cheaper and faster if that underground stream had been discovered before the road was planned. Then the engineers would have evaluated it and put the culvert into the plan from the start. The construction company would not have had to stop and redo parts of the road. It would have handled it as a normal part of the construction.

But physical systems have LP and software is NLP. On our construction site the need for the culvert only impacts the road around it. A few meters of road would have to be torn up, or maybe more, but it's just the bit above that stream. The road 10 kilometers away doesn't suddenly collapse because no one expected to encounter that stream.

AN EXAMPLE OF THE INSEPARABILITY OF DESIGN AND BUILD IN SOFTWARE

Software is different. Let me give you a case study to illustrate what can happen with software specifications, i.e. blueprints.

Let's take a look at a seemingly simple case. You are a programmer, and you have to implement a feature in a system. The description you received from your manager said: *list all the clients who have had at least one invoice since the beginning of the fiscal year (active clients), and who have had at least one invoice over $100,000 (large clients).*

This is a typical kind of "specification" you get. As a non-programmer, it probably sounds specific enough.

But now let's put you in the programmer's seat. You are sitting in front of a computer with the source code opened in an editor in front of you. In the code you already have a list of all the clients. You have to figure out how to come up with this sub-list that has the right clients. You are in luck. There is already one subroutine that picks the active clients out of a list, and another that picks the large clients from a list.

One decision you have to make is: in what order should you do these two selections?

Depending on how things have been set up in the system this might require only two lines of code:

Line 1: Select the active clients
Line 2: From the active clients select the large clients

But you could also do it the other way around:

Line 1: Select the large clients
Line 2: From the large clients select the active clients

You, the programmer, are now doing design work. Should the specification have indicated the order of operations? They never do, because this is seen as programming, and as we shall see, the author of the specification doesn't have enough information to make that decision.

Let us now look at the implications of your design decision.

Two key questions are: how much time does it take to determine if a client is active? And how much time does it take to determine if a client is large?

Let us suppose there will eventually be 10,000 clients where 1% are active, and 1% are large.

To make an initial selection will take 10,000 evaluations of the selection criteria.

Once the first selection has been done there will be about one hundred clients. Therefore the first selection criteria gets evaluated 10 thousand times, while the second criteria is evaluated one hundred times.

Suppose it takes 360 milliseconds (360/1000 of a second) to evaluate one of these criteria for a single client, but only 0.1 microseconds to evaluate the other for a client.

If you put the slower selection first, it will take 3,600 seconds, or one hour.

If you put the quicker selection first it will take 1 millisecond, or $1/1000^{th}$ of a second.

That's a 3.6 million to 1 difference!

The second criteria will only be evaluated 100 times so it will take at most 3 seconds.

So how does a programmer, especially one new to the project, know which option is faster? There could be thousands of lines of code, and it is hard to isolate and time a small sequence when the system is running operationally. Notice that it is only the time these bits of code take when running in actual operations that matters. Quite often, when running a system in test mode the timings are artificially low. It is impossible to efficiently time every little bit of the code, so it is very hard to determine exactly how fast or slow a particular fragment of code will execute when working for real.

Suppose your code is called when someone hits a button. As time goes by, and the number of clients grows, the speed will get slower and slower. Users are generally frustrated by a delay of a few seconds. If it climbs to over 20 seconds they are going to be hitting the button again and again. When it starts going over 40 seconds they will mostly give up. That's if they can. Sometimes the system is not listening to events, like those coming from a keyboard or a mouse, until it completes the task. If that was the case, when the number of clients suddenly ballooned to 10,000 you would find people locked out for an hour while the selection ground away. Can they cancel and start again? Maybe, but that can put the system in an unusual state. Then it's a question of whether those error conditions have been handled correctly by another programmer, who wrote the code that handles situations such as the user terminating a program by using the task manager, or even by powering down the machine.

To try to figure out which should come first, you could start to search through the code for the evaluation of each selection. But that could be layer after layer of code that you didn't write, and you would have to struggle to understand it and all its implications. It could take you a couple of days to really figure out all the things going on in that code and to reach a level of understanding equal to that of the programmer who wrote it.

The original programmer might know that the first selection is a resource hog and would make sure to put it in the right order, but this is the kind of knowledge you lose with staff turnover. It's not written down. The original programmer might have put a comment in the code:

```
// Warning – this is expensive
```

But what is expensive? This routine takes 360 ms, or about 1/3 of a second. If it is just checking a single client, that is fast enough. It's only when the routine gets called 10,000 times that things take too long. Remember, the design is not complete because the software isn't finished, so when the person wrote that function they had no idea it was going to be used in a bulk selection. They just thought they had to put a note up on a client screen to say that they were a large client. In that case 1/3 of a second would be totally acceptable. To put in that comment, the original programmer would have had to be prescient.

Suppose you figure out, or are told, that you should call the operations in a certain order, and you do. That is good, but only as long as the subroutines you are using don't change. Quite often the programmers who are working on a part of the software that deals with clients (for example) are not aware of all ways this code will be used.

Perhaps, after you have made the right choice, things change, and someone else alters those selection sub-routines, so now your right decision becomes the wrong one.

You started out intending to program a small feature, but it required a thorough analysis of the current code and where it might go. That is design. Either you give someone the actual code, or they will be doing design. NLP can cause small design changes to become major stumbling blocks to other system changes. If you try to divide and conquer software you find out that there are all kinds of hidden dependencies that can cause problems. Your little step from one feature set to another may cause some major parts of the software to unravel and throw all of the project estimates into confusion.

Software can't be modeled because if it's not defined at the lower levels then it's not defined at the higher levels. Software is somewhat binary in that regard; it is either totally defined, or it is totally not defined.

SOFTWARE PROJECTS CANNOT SEPARATE DESIGN AND BUILD

Every programmer has experienced the frustration of going to do a simple task and have it unwind.

Let's suppose, for example, you go to add a new monitoring feature which is going to track the traffic in and out of a communications channel. You find that this requires a connection to a communications library, and that the system already uses the maximum number of connections that particular library supports. You realize that a new version of the communications library can handle more connections, so you install that. Unfortunately, the new library has some minor differences in its interface and that causes every place that calls the library to fail. There are several hundred of them.

Bummer! This is where you stare at the screen and snarl at someone, something, anything!

You could go back to the old library, but that isn't going to work. Eventually, for one reason or another, you will have to upgrade. Besides, you have to get this task finished and you can't think of any way of doing it without getting a connection. So, you roll up your sleeves and start looking at the several hundred places the library is called. Unfortunately, the change is not something you can do with a bulk edit, as each one requires you to figure out how to handle it in that situation. You spend three days going through and finding all the places that call that library and fix the calls for the new library. Unfortunately, you accidentally change a line of code while you are doing that and that causes another module to crash randomly. That causes a real panic and you spend two days tracking it down and finally figuring out that it was caused by your fumble-finger mistake while doing the updates. Now, about six days later, you are ready to go back and start the task you wanted to do in the first place.

You might be thinking, "Well, that is just bad design." You could say, "Why didn't you realize that the number of connections to that library was being exceeded? Why didn't you design it to handle the right number of connections in the first place?"

That kind of logic might work when the design is stable, but if the design is fluid, how do you know how many connections you need to that library? Sure, you design some part of code and that functionality will require a connection so you can count it—but what about parts of the code that you didn't realize required a connection. That pushes the question to, "Why didn't you realize that that part of the code required a connection?"

That's a good question—and this is the answer.

Let us suppose we have designed a computer system and we have done what the above questions imply is missing, i.e. we produced a complete specification for the system—a blueprint if you will. So now we should be able to make sure that nothing like running out of connections can happen—right? Well, unfortunately, no.

There are only two possibilities:

1. our lovely design can be turned into a working system by an algorithmic process, or

2. it cannot.

Let us reflect for a moment on what software is. According to the dictionary the definition of software is:

"Instructions in some notational language that can be algorithmically turned into a set of executable machine instructions."

If it can be algorithmically turned into working software then it is something in a notational language that can be turned into a set of executable machine instructions. This means having a specification that is a complete specification of the software you want—then it already *is* the software you want! Wait a second—if the design is essentially the software, then it's going to be as hard to do the design as it is to do the software. This doesn't solve anything. It just moves the implementation of the system to a design phase which is so detailed that you are actually writing code.

If it cannot be turned into a working system by some kind of mechanical step-by-step procedure then we have to examine what is missing. Why can't it be? What is stopping this specification being turned into a system?

What this clearly means is that there are parts of the system that are not specified sufficiently to mechanically build them. That means that their design has not been finalized. This means that programmers have to fill in those design gaps and figure out how to make something work when there is no specification.

This is where NLP comes into play. A small change in a design at some low level can have totally non-local and non-proportional effects. It may be that the way someone implements something at a low level invalidates a major design level elsewhere.

That small change may well be something such as: because the design was not complete, no one realized that a bit of code needed to access a communications channel.

There we go. *All designs for software will be incomplete unless they are actually the software.* If designs are incomplete, then NLP means that designing while one is programming can produce severe impacts in any part of the design.

What this says is that, in software, there is no way to separate the design from the build.

NOT SO AGILE

The methodology-du-jour is called Agile.

Agile says pick a set of small features and implement them at a set constant rate (the "cadence"). This follows the belief that, overall, one can proceed with incremental improvements until the final goal is reached.

The idea is that you always have a working system. It is destabilized only briefly and then brought back to stability. This is completely a physical world mindset: a bit of small functionality must be a small change and a small change can only have small effects. But we know this is not the case in the NLP software world.

Giving up is hard to do, and we humans don't easily relinquish our common sense view, which says that if you can't get control of the whole project, break it up into bite-sized chunks.

This is like the tunnel-boring example we looked at earlier. Divide the tunnel into sections and it will go faster in a very predictable way. Double the number of machines and you double the amount of tunnel you can bore in a day.

You can probably already see that that's not going to work. That small change involves design, and unintended consequence that have no respect for your desire to keep the impacts small and localized to a small section of code. It is a consequence of that physical world mindset, but it is the driving force of most methodologies, especially Agile and all of its various spinoffs. This was also the same approach used by the Spiral methodology which is one I tried when running a project to build a portfolio management system in the 1980s. Spiral was essentially the same as Agile, but with different nomenclature. It didn't work either, and it was abandoned, as I predict Agile will be sometime in the next decade.

The overarching problem is that NLP invalidates this type of approach. The divide-and-conquer strategy is a physical world strategy that doesn't work in software. Because a small portion can't be fully specified until fully built, that may require modifications to other portions, and those impacts may spread to yet other portions. Take our example with the communication connections. Maybe this bit of functionality requires a connection that will overflow the total number of connections and force a new library. What happens if there is no new version that handles more connections? Then you have a problem. You are faced with either building a communications library yourself or redesigning the system to use some other form of communications that doesn't have the same limitation. If you can get the source code of the library (you can if it is open-source—if it's proprietary then you can't) you have a shot at being able to modify it. However, you may not have the expertise to do that. Even if you do, there is no guarantee that the source code you have to modify is not high entropy, and it's going to be a long and frustrating time to get your modifications working. We can see that a small stumbling block like running out of connections can spiral you into a cascading world of hurt. So much for "Agile's cadence," and releasing working software at specified intervals. So much for agility. Your quick fix turned into a stumbling, clumsy hack through thorny vines.

The scientific method is to form a hypothesis and then test it with experimentation. In contrast, these methodologies are "one-step" science. That is, they are all hypothesis and no experimentation. The problem is that it is impossible to really compare two approaches to software development. The outcomes are so tied up with the abilities of the programmers that unless you clone the whole team you are not going to get a meaningful comparison. Having the same team redo a project doesn't work either, because the second time around the team is not the same team that did the project the first time—they are more experienced in general and have actual experience in that particular system. Not only is the team different, but the software you use has moved on. There are new libraries, new languages. As Heraclitus said, *"No man ever steps into the same river twice"*.

You cannot restrain the impacts of a small bit of functionality. Unless you fully implement that functionality, you won't be able to predict all of the impacts it could have on different parts of the system.

This just doesn't sit well with a lot of people, especially non-programming managers. They want to run their projects as if they were physical projects. All our physical world common sense keeps telling us that we can nail down the top levels and sweat the details later. All software development methodologies come down to this, and that is why they have all failed. They have failed because software does not behave like physical systems. Those who are trying to evangelize software development methodologies like Agile are stuck in a physical world mind set.

METHODOLOGIES ARE SNAKE OIL

What all this says is that software methodologies are provable nonsense, and anyone trying to sell you one, or sell you training for one, is selling you snake oil.

I'm not saying that you shouldn't have a careful approach to building software, but every project is unique and requires the right, specific architecture, which dictates how it should be built. Like the design, the methodology is inseparable from the programming.

The Agile methodology is following the path of all belief-based systems. The inevitable breaking into factions has happened with Agile, with Scrum, XP, Kanban, and Crystal as just a few of the dazzling array of Agile spin-offs.

One of the original authors of the Agile manifesto, Dave Thomas, has said *"Agile has become a marketing term for anyone with points to espouse, hours to bill, or products to sell."* After all, methodologies are very profitable, and who doesn't want to get their software finished on time? This is fertile ground to charge a lot of money to deliver something with dubious value.

So as far as methodologies go, the only thing approaching a methodology that I found some sense in was a concept by IBM called "Chief Programmer Team." This is analogous to a surgical team.

The head of a surgical team is a surgeon. They are the one doing the surgery, and the rest of the team is composed of assistants, who might take care of specialized tasks or body areas, like the anesthesiologist, or para-surgical staff such as nurses and technicians. In the same way, the head of a project team should be a programmer[13] who can implement his or her vision of the top-level architecture.

Software is just fundamentally different from physical systems and running software projects like physical projects and trying to break them into smaller manageable pieces just doesn't work. This hasn't stopped

---

[13] This could be because I'm a programmer and I always run my projects that way. I admit to a bias.

methodology mavens from continually trying, promoting methodology after methodology, each one of which is trumpeted as being the solution to software project problems.

Given that this has been going on, unabated, for nearly 60 years, it shows how hard it is to give up the comforts of common sense developed in the physical world, and actually face the fact that software is different.

Yet there are more factors that make software different than the physical world. Where most manufacturing and production has been heavily automated, this is absolutely not true about software, as we shall see in the next chapter.

SOFTWARE PATENTS ARE LOGICAL NONSENSE

Before we get to concept of programming as a purely human activity, I also want to add a comment about software patents. Patents supposedly are a way of preserving methods and techniques for public use by granting an exclusive license for a fixed period of time to the inventor. In the physical world this prevents inventors resorting to trade secrets to protect their innovation and hence denying that knowledge to society as a whole.

Lawyers have naively pushed that concept into the software world not realizing that software is very different and that software patents, like software methodologies are logically nonsensical.

To try to describe software so that you can patent it is to fail to realize that no description of software is complete unless it is the software itself. This is clearly the realm of copyright which recognizes that the whole work is the intellectual property and not some abbreviated description of it.

Patenting software is like patenting literature. Can you imagine getting a patent for a concept such as "a book that has one person taking the place of another who is condemned to the guillotine." Every author alive today could write such a book, and each one would be different, and none of them would be *A Tale of Two Cities*.

Software patents are crude descriptions of software that are not complete enough to describe the exact software, which makes it impossible to determine infringement. This is a goldmine for patent trolls and lawyers as this imprecision makes it possible to use software patents to extort money from companies who may be using something that looks a bit like whatever it is that is described in the patent.

Large companies gather together massive collections of patents to ward off patent trolls and large competitors much as someone in a movie gathers garlic and crosses to ward off vampires. It is basically immaterial as to what those patents are, as pretty much any software patent can be used to claim infringement in almost any circumstance.

This is a huge drag on innovation, especially for small companies. That, of course, works to the advantage of large companies and further perpetuates profitable monopolies. And, of course, the lawyers make money from all sides.

9
WRITING SOFTWARE
IS A PURELY HUMAN ACTIVITY

I was a young sophomore in 1963. Because I had taken first-year university math in high school, I was taking third-year math courses. One course was on numerical analysis, and in order to do the various calculations required, we spent the first three weeks of the course learning computer programming.

To write my first program, I went into the engineering building that had half of the third floor devoted to an IBM 7040 computer. It had an air-conditioned room to itself and was attended by a staff of operators. Lowly undergraduates like me were not allowed near this (to me) almost mythical machine. I had always wanted to program a computer and had spent a lot of my spare time in high school building various logic circuits.

There was a room where you could sit down at a table and write out your programs. It was quiet, with everyone frowning in concentration. I got a pad of coding sheets. These were green, lined sheets where every line was marked off in 80 columns which was the number of characters a punched card held. I had sketched out the algorithm I was going to program. It was a simple program to find the largest number in a list of numbers. In pencil, I carefully wrote my program line by line. I read it over carefully, following the logic in my head, trying to convince myself that it would do what I wanted it to do. Then I took the two pages of my program and found a free keypunch machine in the "unit record" room of the computer center. I fed a stack of blank yellow "FORTRAN" cards into the hopper and started typing in my program. Each carriage return would slide the card across and add it to the stack of completed cards. When I was finished I took the card deck and fed it into a listing machine. This read the cards and printed out the lines. The text was also printed on top of the cards but that was hard to read when trying to see if your program was correct.

I took the printout back to the room and studied it carefully. When I was convinced it would work I wrapped a rubber band around the card deck and put it into the one-hour tray. Later in the day I came back to find the printed output wrapped around my card deck and secured by a rubber band.

The printout would list my program and tell me if there were any errors in the code, in which case the program was stopped at that point. If the compiler passed my code, then it was run by the computer and the output was printed after the program listing.

This was a slow process. If I made a mistake in the programming, even just a comma out of place, it came back with an error message and I had to re-punch some cards to correct the error and resubmit it in the one-hour tray.

However, despite the crude way of entering the program and the slow turnaround, if I still had a copy of this program it would run on today's computers using the latest 2015 version of Fortran. It would run faster, but it would produce exactly the same output[14].

---

[14] All computer languages have a fanatical determination to maintain backward compatibility. Once a language achieves wide-spread usage it is absolutely essential for newer versions not to invalidate the billions of lines of existing code that a huge number of organizations depend on.

If I was to code this program in one of the languages I use today, such as Java, I would be doing almost exactly what I did 55 years ago. That is, I would sit down in front of a keyboard, and in my mind form a representation of the algorithm. Then I would think of what statements in the language I would have to write so that the program executed the algorithm.

The hardware is very different. I could never have dreamed back then of typing using a colored video screen and being able to compile and run my program in seconds, rather than putting a deck of cards in a tray and waiting hours for the output. But the programming activity is very similar. By the time the 1970s came around pretty much everything we use today had been thought of, we just had primitive versions. We had file sharing on remote computers, we were using video terminals (even if they were monochrome), and the first start of the Internet. Even color graphics were available on specialized, and highly expensive, hardware. All the computer languages and operating systems we use today were started in the 1950s, '60s and '70s, or had precursors created in those decades [15].

This surprises most people when I explain it to them. They have assumed that modern software development is as different from 1970s software development as modern medicine differs from 1970s medicine—when antibiotics were used with abandon, ulcers were thought to be caused by diet, and all medical equipment had analog meter needles and lights, instead of modern digital graphics.

---

[15] MacOS is based on BSD Unix, and Unix was created in 1969. Linux started from GNU Unix. MSDOS started as a clone of CP/M which was created in 1974 and was heavily influenced by DECs TOPS-10 created in 1964. Windows is really just a graphics interface on top of MSDOS. Although you could argue that Windows 10 is a direct descendant of Windows NT, that was done in the 1980s based on 1970s work by DEC.

That is just not the case. Even though today I program using a really good development environment, and my machine is many orders of magnitude faster than the ones I started on, I could put 1970s me to work on some parts of my project immediately, with no training.

When I open a terminal window[16] on any Windows, Mac or Linux machine, I get a screen that looks just like a 1970s terminal. It hasn't changed in 40 years. Sure, I have all kinds of options for background and text color, but if I leave it as white text on a black background it looks just exactly like a 1970s video terminal, and 1970s me would feel right at home. It not only looks like a 1970s video terminal, with flashing cursor and monospaced font, it is ready to execute the same Unix commands that I was using in the 1970s. If I wanted that prior me to build a utility script for moving files around in some way, I would just have to describe it and he would be on it. No training necessary. In the world of command line scripts which control the world's servers, nothing much has changed.

If I wanted 1970s me to work on my main code base, which is in Java, I would have to take him through the Java language. It uses the same layout conventions as the C language, which was invented in the early '70s. It is object oriented which is a programming paradigm first implemented in Sumula67. By the 1970s I had written programs in all kinds of languages and operating systems. Learning a new computer language is not really a big deal; it was, and still is, a continual part of my programming life. It would take me a few hours to get that prior me to start programming and, in a week, he would be flying along.

---

[16] You can do this on a Mac by running the terminal application. On Windows you can run a command prompt. If you're using Linux you already know.

Of all the technical disciplines, programming has changed the least. The concept of figuring out an algorithm and then typing text hasn't changed since the 1950s. We have better tools today, but they are only incrementally better. I don't have to wait for output from the one-hour tray to come back—now my compiles take seconds to do it in front of my eyes. There are many more languages now, all fighting for dominance, but fundamentally the programming process is the same. It's just: think how you can do the task, in the language you have, and then type it in. As errors are discovered, correct and repeat.

So why is this? Why has software development had such a curious pattern—a massive explosion in the first few decades, and then just incremental changes for all the following decades?

This is all a result of NLP. We saw in the previous chapter that because of NLP we have no way of modeling software. It isn't decomposable to independent parts as a physical system is. Its design is not decomposable and hence a design is never totally finished until the software is totally finished.

So, as we have seen, that means that programming always involves design. If you give a programmer a design it won't be complete, because if it was, why wouldn't you just turn it into code mechanically? You can't, because there isn't enough information in the design to specify the entire system. Something or someone has to provide that extra design. That entity has to craft an algorithm that hopefully will accomplish something that gets closer to a finished system.

The only entity that can do that is a human being. So human beings are absolutely essential to programming. The human mind is what interprets whatever information it has about the system into actual statements in a programming language.

There have been many attempts to produce software that could program other software, but except for a few specialized cases, this effort has been a total failure. Management has always wanted to get rid of programmers because they give bad estimates and continually create bugs, but despite every attempt, as you read this book millions of human programmers are at their desks typing away or staring with puzzlement at a screen, wondering what caused an error.

Everything that goes into a software system is passed through the mind of a human programmer and typed in as text via a keyboard. This total human dependency makes software totally different from a physical system.

Software is the exclusive domain of the human mind.

Consider the impacts of this. If you have a programming team, it doesn't matter what kind of documentation you have if the programmers don't read it. It doesn't matter what kind of orders you give if they don't really listen. Anything that is entered into that software is done because a programmer on the team thinks they are improving the system.

Now the key word there is "thinks." This is purely a subjective decision by the programmer, based on what information they have absorbed about the project. They can be reading a design document that is specifying a screen layout, but they are going to have to build all the code around it and convince themselves that their code will have the desired effect. Of course, this depends on the accuracy of their mental information. If they have misread something, or if they are confused about something, those misconceptions will be incorporated into the code.

In the physical world things are very different. Take the compressor blade of a jet engine. There is a design that specifies its shape, with mathematical equations and measurements down to micrometers. It totally defines a turbine blade for this engine. In this case the value rests in the design. The design can be mechanically turned into an actual turbine blade by using robotic milling machines. Even if we use human machinists they will produce the exact same shape. The fact that one of them has a hangover won't impact the shape of the turbine blade—unless it is improperly machined—but physical systems are measurable, so every blade can be checked and any that do not meet standards can be discarded. This means that the impact of the state of any of the operators is removed at this point in the process. The problem is totally local and there is a strict specification filter that stops any non-compliant turbine blades entering the rest of the system.

Things in the physical world are measurable. You can measure work that is done and see if it complies with the design. But no one has ever figured out how to measure software, and forget trying to see if it complies with the design, because there was no complete design in the first place. Again, if there was a complete design, it would be able to be executed and hence it would be a program.

Whenever a programmer comes to accomplish a task there are a huge number of ways it can be done. That applies at any level. Even if a programmer is trying to decide something simple such as how to sort a list of items, there are scores of options, each one having different speed and storage characteristics. How exactly a programmer implements something depends on their programming style, the project coding standards (if there are any and if the programmer knows them), and limitations of the particular software environment they are working in. If you have five people implement the same feature, you will get five different approaches.

How careful they are can depend a lot on fatigue. When you're tired, doing the code the right way (i.e. doing a lot of repetitive exception-handling code) can feel like too much effort, so you leave it, intending to come back to it later. Programmers often do something quickly to test if it works. They don't want to put in a lot of comments and error handling in case it doesn't work and they have to rewrite it some other way. The intention to come back and fix it properly is quite often forgotten, especially if the project is under intense pressure to get things done. My grandfather always used to say that the road to hell is paved with good intentions.

It is very common for this kind of rushed approach to create code where error exceptions are ignored. When the code is left in this quick-and-dirty state it can cause problems. Suppose this code is part of the backup subsystem. Because of the lack of error handling when an error condition is encountered the program does nothing. It does not alert anyone, it just silently stops and doesn't do the backup. It can be a nasty surprise when you need that backup.

What contributes to these kinds of errors? Stress, certainly will, as will lack of knowledge, and unfamiliarity with this project. You can see that software systems are different from physical systems in this regard. In physical systems we can separate the design from the build, we can give the people who will build the physical thing a complete specification and that means we can replace members of the build team without undue impact on the project.

In physical systems there is also a clear status divide between designers and builders. Architects can be world famous. Contractors, carpenters and plumbers are often considered "mere" tradespeople, with no real input into the creative aspects of the process.

This is the complete reverse of a software project. In a software project there may be an architect/designer, but a large amount of design work ends up being done by the programming team. Very often in a software project what is finally built is very different from what was originally envisioned. In software projects there is no separation between designer and builder. There is less of a status distinction as well. Some people trumpet themselves, or have titles of software architect, in order to gain some of the status of those jobs in the physical world, but a programmer who builds a significant project is recognized as being invaluable to the project.

We can see that programming is unique in the technical disciplines. It is totally and absolutely a human activity that cannot be automated. It is totally reliant on the programmer's skill, their knowledge and their mental state.

SOFTWARE PROJECT ENTROPY

As programming is such a human activity, and so much knowledge is held in human minds as opposed to documents, the concept of entropy has to be extended to the entire system, which includes the programmers. It is this combined system that produces the code. Any entropy in any part of this combination will cause problems.

First, what is a software project? It consists of:

1. the source code
2. the computing environment which includes the hardware used, the computer language used and the various software tools
3. the programmers

Any entropy in any of the parts of a software project will add to the total project entropy and increase the probability of having an error.

Bugs in the software are going to cause problems. If the source code has been hacked and slashed by many different programmers and chopped and changed by moving specifications and management indecision, it will be high entropy and continually produce errors.

If the computing environment is deficient this will add to project entropy. I have seen this mainly in the case of skimping on the hardware. You see companies paying lots of money for software but giving the users old computers. Given the low cost of really capable hardware, this is penny-wise and pound-foolish. You should try to make sure that your hardware is far more capable than the minimum configuration. There are all kinds of errors that are triggered by slow or low-storage hardware.

For example, when memory is low the software may be designed to kick other things out of memory to make room. This takes the software down paths that are rarely executed. If the hardware is slow it puts the software into very different behavior patterns, and although it shouldn't make a difference, it often triggers bugs that had not previously been encountered. If disk space is low then the program may fail because certain files can't be created. These kinds of problems can be hard to diagnose because they are so local to a particular machine and what it is running at the time.

I recently had a client who was resisting upgrading a 4GB machine to 8GB. Given that, as of the time of writing this, 8GB is the minimum memory on a back-to-school special, it is hard to see the rationale for this kind of decision. When you look at the high cost and uncertainty of technical support and compare it to the low cost and certainty of hardware, it just doesn't make a lot of sense.

Finally, there are the programmers. Unlike physical systems, where most of the knowledge is in the design, in software systems a large amount of the knowledge rests with the programmers. It is a generally accepted fact in software that the best person to maintain a program is the person who wrote it.

Think of our example about Bill the intern, who sat down at Steve's desk. Steve knew that he was working on some special debugging code and wouldn't have made the same mistake. But when he abruptly left the project, the knowledge was lost. Bill should have been better handled, but if the project is under time pressure and there are lots of emergencies going on that kind of thing is precisely what happens. You can see that disorder can create further disorder. If the project was calmer, and people were being logical in their behavior, perhaps someone could have shut down Steve's computer properly. Failing that, they could have listened to Bill's questions when he was confronted with a logged-in user.

Stress is a form of entropy. Humans are incapable of writing error-free code, but humans trying to rush to get something/anything working create far more errors.

This is not true of physical projects. Stress can cause an uptick in accidents and mistakes that have to be corrected, but because of years of training and the repetitive and well-defined tasks that they do, trades people usually do a professional job, regardless of stress. Also, remember that mistakes made in a physical system are local in effect. If an electrician mistakenly hooks the ground to the hot wire, it will pop a circuit breaker. It is an effect directly connected to the wiring mistake, and easily fixed. It won't cause the plumbing to start leaking inside a wall somewhere else in the building.

When Steve left, some of the project knowledge left with him. In a physical project it would be like someone leaving the construction site and taking a piece of the only copy of the blueprint with them. There is just some knowledge about the software that cannot be captured by documentation. That is why the only real way that programmers are trained is by mentoring[17].

Staff turnover is a huge contributor to project entropy. Working on a software project is a learning experience. Over time you start to get a good picture of how the whole system works, how the different parts communicate. If you leave the project, that knowledge you spent a long time gaining goes with you.

Just because the project has significant documentation doesn't mean that it helps, because a programmer has to read it and understand it so it can be applied to programming or debugging. If people are added to a project in a structured way, and are given seminars on the project, and time to review the documentation (if it exists), then they have a much better chance of not creating problems when they start programming. Of course, a project in panic mode just can't do that. When projects are in a panic they just throw people in at the deep end.

To be fair to project management, a lot of programmers don't have the patience to methodically come up to speed on a project. Certainly, in the past, I have been guilty of that. I just wanted to get to the code and figure it out on the fly.

PROJECT ENTROPY

These are massive contributors to project entropy:

1. adding new people to a project
2. removing people from a project
3. subjecting project programmers to stress
4. having management stuck in physical world mindset.

---

[17] Programming is our closest modern version of the guild system. Beginning programmers (apprentices) are mentored until they are "experienced" (journeyman) and then if they continue to program they become "expert" (master).

We saw in the story of Bill the intern that entropy increased when Steve left, and Bill joined for a few minutes. It was a combination of the unusual state of Steve's computer with Bill's lack of knowledge. Also, Steve would have had a better chance of diagnosing the problem if he had remained with the project. It was the project stress that started all of this.

Entropy is the main killer of systems, as we shall see in later chapters when we explore more of the hidden software world. Systems can enter an "entropy death spiral," or become a "zombie" system. This can happen to any system if care is not taken to control entropy.

This is true of all software. So why does enterprise software fail so much more often, when other kinds of software, like aerospace systems or word processors seem so much more successful? That is the topic of the next chapter.

10
ENTERPRISE SYSTEMS ARE REALLY HARD

In the early 1980s I was working for an aerospace company that was a world leader in building satellite ground stations. These ingenious combinations of hardware and software could show images in real time, so watching the screen was like being in the satellite, looking down as the earth passed below you. This was done in a time when computers were about a million times slower than today. It required very involved software to work with specialized hardware to squeeze out every bit of performance possible. This was a company that was highly skilled in writing complex software.

One of their senior engineers had landed a contract with a local airline to help plan their flights. Using a Perkin Elmer (Interdata) minicomputer and writing in assembler code he produced a simple system and installed it at the airline's nearby head office. It was very successful in planning much more efficient routes and saving a measurable amount of money.

Many large, European airlines took notice and contracted for a system to be built for their airlines. Of course, they wanted a lot of extra features. During the contract negotiations the aerospace company was pleased that the airlines were quite willing to pay, and pay well, for these planned, extra features. This was a pleasant contrast to the mainly government clients they had had so far who were chronically under-funded and were always trying to get extra features for free.

The final list of capabilities was quite ambitious, far beyond the really simple system that had been so successful at the small, local airline. It required keeping track of many statistics, such as: average fuel consumption per kilometer, weather conditions, and passenger counts. All of this data had to be aggregated over time and reported on. It was an enterprise system.

The whole project was predicated on using new mini-computers. It made it so much cheaper than using one of those giant IBM mainframes, that several airlines signed contracts for the system. Of course, all of these airlines had different requests for features. The sales team was delighted to negotiate a generous price for all of these extra features.

They started hiring programmers to do all of this work and the team grew. There were missed deadlines and tensions flared. As time went on things became worse, and more and more people were hired. Soon it was the largest project in the company, and soon after that it was larger than the whole rest of the company put together.

The project team was baffled by the seemingly endless series of problems. A year went by, and then another, and then another. The customers went from understanding, to annoyed, to downright hostile. The money had long run out and the company was now funding the project, which was burning through all the revenue from the aerospace projects. A once-profitable company started charging its employees for coffee.

Finally, the inevitable happened. The project was cancelled, and the clients were given whatever software had been written so far. That they didn't sue was probably because what little money was left in a near-bankrupt aerospace company was minor to a large airline. To them it was just not worth all the effort and expense that suing would have cost. The aerospace company, teetering on bankruptcy, was acquired, and fresh money put in. The new owners wisely concentrated on aerospace and the failed project faded into corporate memory as a bad dream.

At the time I was quite struck by the calm arrogance of the engineers who assumed that they could easily do an enterprise system. After all, in enterprise systems the calculations you are doing are mostly additions, with the occasional multiplication. They were people who routinely handled the complex mathematics of Fourier transforms and signal processing. They just didn't realize that the complexity of making data from different periods combine with new data and keep a continual flow of reports can be immense. Staggered by the way the project kept on going, with no end in sight, they did the worst possible thing and started throwing new people at it. Predictably the entropy increased as these new people were trying to get up to speed and taking time away from all the other programmers. The system just didn't stabilize and deadline after deadline was missed.

They didn't realize that their complicated ground stations were specialized machines that did only one job. It took an exactly-defined flow of data from a satellite and displayed it as an image. You just kept on testing and testing on the reams of satellite data available until it worked well enough to ship. It didn't have to accumulate data and run complex reports, giving all kinds of views of the data. The satellite never changed, so the imaging worked as long as it was up there. In contrast, airlines are continually changing. They were and are a ferociously-regulated industry, and they have to change with the regulator's directives at the regulator's schedule. During the development project the clients were making continual change requests.

This was all high entropy. Pressure on the team caused stress. There was turnover on the project as some people quit to go somewhere less crazy. There was a continual flow of new people. They were just thrown into the project and told to code. Predictably they made many mistakes that further slowed things down. This system never saw the light of day; it died stillborn. The massive amount of project entropy created a situation where there was never anything close to a working system.

Enterprise computing just seems pedestrian when compared to the wonders of software that circles Jupiter returning scientific data, the marvels of software that identifies animals in images, and the coolness of software that creates virtual 3D worlds around you. None of those adjectives like "wonderful", "marvelous", or "cool" is ever used to describe enterprise software.

I'm sure your impression of enterprise software is that of boring things that deliver needed information. If you are involved in any way with enterprise software, you probably see it as an inefficient and unreliable. In short, a continual source of frustration.

What is it about enterprise systems? Everyone else seems to be able to make software that works. So why is enterprise so different? You may think that other organizations are much better at putting in systems than you are. There are people writing software that controls robots on Mars, and your company can't get correct reports out on time. What is going on?

ENTERPRISE SYSTEMS ARE THE HARDEST

The first thing to realize is that enterprise software is by far the hardest software to write. Now I know that sounds incredible, because it runs directly opposite to conventional wisdom. How can adding up numbers and producing reports be as hard to do as programming image recognition, or writing software to control nuclear power plants?

I can tell you, out of personal experience. I have written every kind of software there is. As I mentioned, I once worked for an aerospace company. I wrote software to calculate the exact antenna position for an imaging radar satellite. This was done by calculating the Doppler shifts in the data being reflected from the ground. The point directly below the satellite was the slowest moving point relative to the satellite, and hence we could find the mid-point in those Doppler shifts. It was more accurate than using the telemetry data. There was a lot of physics involved, and it all had to be implemented in software in a way that could come up with the most accurate measurement. That sounds highly technical and complicated. The theory behind it was, but once all the equations had been developed it was not a super-hard programming task. It was far easier than any enterprise software I have ever done.

I have worked on computer simulations and mathematical optimizations. I have also built computer language parsers, written device drivers, designed communications protocols, written parts of operating systems, and analyzed musical harmony. Combining all that with the large number of enterprise systems I've written, it means that I've worked on pretty much every kind of software. So what software is the hardest? Without hesitation I would say enterprise software.

There is a lot of arrogance among software programmers. We all think we are the best and can do anything when it comes to computers. In my experience there is nothing like trying to write an enterprise system to teach a programmer some humility.

But why is this? To examine this question, we have to look at the different types of software.

DIFFERENT TYPES OF SOFTWARE

You may have noticed that in all the previous chapters where I talked about the NLP principle of software and about entropy, I didn't distinguish between enterprise software and any other kind of software. That is because these are attributes of all software.

However, in this book I am talking about enterprise software failure and what causes it. This raises a question: if these software attributes are at the heart of the failure of enterprise systems, why doesn't this extend to all software? Why isn't all software experiencing the same rate of expensive and highly public failures as enterprise software?

To examine these issues, we can divide software into four different types:

1. Scientific and Engineering software
2. Packaged Software
3. Browser-Based Cloud Software
4. Enterprise Systems

Taking each one in its turn:

SCIENTIFIC AND ENGINEERING SOFTWARE

This covers all the aerospace programming such as the Mars Lander or the Cassini mission. It covers all the process control systems in power plants and electrical grids. It includes all the engineering analysis done to design brides, buildings, and dams. I'm also throwing AI, robotics, 3D printing, and voice processing in here as well. Also, all the operating systems stuff along with communications and encryption.

PACKAGED SOFTWARE

The most prominent example of packaged software is Microsoft's Office suite. This category also includes graphic art programs such as Adobe Illustrator and Photoshop. It includes all the business software, like QuickBooks, and a myriad of other programs that are purchased in some manner by users. The common thread here is that this software is in effect "certified" by the manufacturer, as they put their brand on it and hence their reputation.

I include some so-called "cloud solutions" in this category as well. For example, Adobe Creative Suite (now called Creative Cloud) does not work in a browser but requires installation of the program that talks to the cloud. The word cloud here is just advertising. It's installed software like any other packaged software; it just happens to access the cloud heavily. It also tends to update itself with or without user permission. This kind of software is sometimes charged for by a monthly subscription, but that is just billing practice and doesn't impact the issues we are considering.

Microsoft Office 365 is similar to the Adobe product, it is basically software that updates automatically. In both cases, data can be stored on remote servers, but that is really conceptually no different than storing it on a local hard drive or a company hard drive on a server in your office.

BROWSER-BASED CLOUD SOFTWARE

This software works in a browser. Browsers are separate programs written by various groups. At present there are five major browsers: Chrome, Firefox, Safari, Internet Explorer, and Edge. A browser, as you are probably aware, is a program that connects via the internet to web servers. These provide a computing environment that websites can have fine control over, and hence come close to the quality of native programs. The software is delivered every time the user connects, so it can be updated on the fly.

ENTERPRISE SYSTEMS SOFTWARE

This is the focus of the discussion in this book. In this category we include such software systems as the Phoenix payroll system and the systems you use in your own organization, such as the ERP systems from the major vendors like SAP, Oracle, and Microsoft. Basically, this is software that is integrated into the normal operations of an enterprise.

What makes the first three different from enterprise software? Why are they able to produce stable software and enterprise is not?

RELEVANT FACTORS

There are differences in the ways each of these types of software are developed, tested, and deployed. There are three relevant factors that influence how things are done and the frequency of software failure:

CONTROL OVER FEATURES

Does the project team have the final say when it comes to features and changes? Do they have to consult with an outside constituency?

GENERIC OR CONSTANT TEST DATA

How do you generate test data? Can the project team generate sufficient coverage or do they require data from actual operations?

CHANGE OVER TIME

Does the software have to change its logic over time, yet still preserve existing information?

SCIENTIFIC AND ENGINEERING SOFTWARE

Take a programmer writing software to plot the path of a spacecraft travelling out in the solar system, flying by several planets. The equations of gravity have to be continually applied to predict the spacecraft's path. Some relativistic effects may have to be taken into account. It is complicated mathematics, and requires tricky algorithms, but one thing is true: the laws of physics don't change and the orbital paths of the planets don't change. The position of a planet will be exactly where it has been calculated to be at the time of the mission.

This means that the software can be run, and run, and run again, each time starting from the same point in time, which determines exactly the position and motion of all the planets and any other bodies we may be taking into account.

When I wrote software for a radar imaging system, I could take some archived satellite data and run my software and look at the results. I could keep doing this until it was giving me seemingly correct answers. Then I could process the image and check the fidelity.

I didn't have to worry about the format of the satellite data changing, or the laws of physics changing. It was totally repeatable and predictable.

And testing was straightforward. I could grab any part of the satellite data I wanted and image it. Analyzing the image indicated how more accuracy in antenna positioning improved the resolution of the image. This meant that there was a massive amount of data that I could use for testing readily available.

It is relatively easy to test engineering and scientific programs because the laws of physics never change and the data sets are always valid and usable for testing. The aerospace company who had failed miserably on an enterprise project had no trouble testing their ground stations. There were huge amounts of data available in a strict, never-changing format. These scientific/technical systems tend to be one-off; a single mission perhaps, or the analysis of a particular bridge.

The amazing reliability of aerospace programs is achieved by relentless testing. Aerospace projects test their software again and again and again. They realize that because of NLP, if you make any change you have to totally retest everything. This has become standard policy for any QA (Quality Assurance, i.e. testing) department. So, this kind of software is easy to test because good test cases are readily available.

In technical/engineering software, decisions on changes almost always rest with the project team. For example, say they have a data entry screen. The information that is gathered is totally determined by the team to ensure that they have enough data and options to do the calculations. They decide how best to lay out that screen, and what options should be on it. They make these decisions based on the technology and how it should be controlled. These are decisions made within the team with very little input from external sources.

Most of this kind of software is used for a single case at a time. You run an analysis of a dam, or a bridge, or you have one space mission. It is normally for one particular situation. If it is modified, a whole new version is produced. The new version might require a different format of data but there is rarely a need to be able to work on the old data.

When you look at the three factors as they apply to scientific/engineering software you can see that:

- Scientific/engineering systems are very much in the control of the project team.
- The test data is normally readily available.
- They don't have to handle changes as well as operate with previous data.

All of this makes scientific/engineering systems less difficult than they might seem on the surface.

PACKAGED SOFTWARE

In the 1990s I was an owner/partner of Paradigm Development Corporation, a contract-software house that did a lot of work for Microsoft, among other large software companies. We wrote file format converters for MS Word and Excel and wrote other utilities and add-ons. One project we had was to remove unused lines in the MS Word code base. It can be hard to know in a large, high-entropy code base if lines of code are actually used. Because parts of the code could modify other parts of the code, it required an engineer to carefully walk through the code to see if a particular block of code was ever used. These blocks of unused, abandoned code are like an industrial plant having machines that are never used and gathering dust, but are getting in the way of normal operations. This is entropy.

The MS Word code base was high entropy. That is not surprising given that, even in the mid-1990s, it was at least a decade old and had been worked on by a continually changing group of programmers.

But you may be thinking, "MS Word works well." Perhaps you use it yourself. It's stable and gets the job done without a massive amount of computer errors.

So how does a high-entropy code base result in a stable product?

It's all about testing. MS has a huge QA team who are relentless in testing. Throughout the development cycle QA are testing and reporting bugs. Bit by bit, over time, the bugs are largely squashed, and the remaining bugs are deemed to be minor enough that they can live with them.

At this point the code is frozen, and a last round of testing is done. If anything new comes up, it is fixed and the software is completely retested. This is because everyone knows that any change has NLP and could cause a major problem. Any change, no matter how minor, should cause a complete redo of QA. This is just QA 101.

Of course, sometimes shortcuts are taken in what are deemed to be low-risk changes, but there are many disaster stories of people who make a last-minute change that "couldn't possibly cause any problems." At Aldus (the company that made PageMaker before being acquired by Adobe) an engineer made a minor change that seemed not to impact anything, but he didn't walk across the street to test on an actual high-end printer. The software failed to print properly on that kind of printer, which was commonly used all over the world. This was in the days when software was being shipped on CDs. Half a million CDs had to be remade and sent as replacements. The engineer was fired.

It is these kinds of stories that make everyone in the packaged software world intensely focused on testing and making sure that the complete test suite is run on all software before it is shipped, no matter how small the last fix was.

This doesn't necessarily mean they have reduced the entropy of the code. They may have rewritten some areas that were particularly bad, but in general they had just found a ledge on the steep slope of system stability. By hammering at the testing and making sure that all the thousands of bugs are inconsequential or manageable they can produce a shippable version.

MS Word, for example, ships with thousands of bugs. These are entries on the bug list that QA has agreed are not bad enough to stop the release. As I write this book using MS Word, small bugs show up. For example, when I scroll up and down with a multi-column view, sometimes a line of text is duplicated. Just scrolling up and then down will force a redraw, and it goes away. If

I don't notice that there are two identical lines and try to edit it, I get some strange behavior with the cursor misplaced but forcing a redraw cleans it all up.

No doubt that bug is somewhere in Microsoft's list and was probably there for a number of releases. It may have been fixed in a later version, but when the version I'm using was released it was deemed acceptable.

Packaged software is in effect, certified. We trust software from a reputable manufacture like Microsoft, or Apple, or Intuit. This is because we know they thoroughly test their software. While that doesn't guarantee you won't have some problems, they will probably be minor and usually there is a work-around.

But notice there is one thing about the testing of packaged software that really makes it easier.

Take testing word processing software for example. A document is a document. It doesn't matter what the actual words are, they could be "Lorem ipsum"[18]. What matters for testing is how the software handles the general word processing characteristics of a document, things like: very long words, paragraphs that take up more than a page, multiple columns, pagination, and footnotes. The actual text is immaterial.

So, testing packaged software is not as hard as it could be. Microsoft maintains a library of test documents and word processing actions. These documents form an incredibly rich set of test data that pits the new version of the software against every problem they've logged before, and a whole set of specially-generated samples of extreme conditions.

An office suite is a set of tools to be used by large numbers of different people to author content, whether it is a presentation deck or a spreadsheet. There is noth-

---

[18] This is Latin that is used by printers to just show example text. Confusingly it is called 'greek'.

ing in the software that is specialized for a particular user—everything is general, and hence can be tested with a generalized test set.

This is not to say that it isn't difficult to bring packaged software to a state that QA will agree to ship. It's incredibly difficult and frustrating, just not as hard as enterprise.

The features of a package like MS Word are totally determined by the project team. Certainly, marketing gets involved and introduces customer needs and wishes but if the team is up against a deadline, some of those feature requests get cut in the interest of getting the product shipped. These decisions are made by the project team. Marketing might object, but if the project team says they can't get it done on time they will win the argument. If the programmers say a feature has to be implemented in a certain way for technical reasons, they win that argument too.

Packaged software is shipped with a clear set of capabilities. These don't change until the next release. This means that new features can be done in the time between releases. The data may not be compatible from one release to another and may therefore require an import program to move from an old release to a new one. But there is no requirement to have new feature code work on both old and new data.

When you look at the three factors as they apply to packaged software you can see that:

- The project team decides on features. There is always input by marketing but the team has final say.

- Testing is made much easier because there is the ability to have a large test suite.

- New features don't have to work with old data.

CLOUD

Subscription software is a new entrant, made possible by the great improvements in communication speed and the adoption of a common communications protocol—i.e. the Internet.

In this model of software delivery, the supplier runs servers that are accessible over the Internet ("the cloud") and clients run software on their local computer to display information on the screen and allow input.

The client is charged on a subscription basis for the use of the software.

Clearly one of the characteristics of this model is that the software can be continually updated (which some might describe as subscription software's biggest advantage and its biggest weakness). However, the current approach to this is to develop a Minimum Viable Product (MVP). This means software with the smallest number of features that is still of enough value to attract a large number of customers. This MVP has to be built and tested. To get to MVP you have to get that minimal amount of stuff working, and you have to test it thoroughly. This is almost identical to packaged software at this point. You have a team and you build and test until you have a MVP, then you put it up for download, or make a website for browser execution, which is a release.

All of the decisions about features are made by the project team. This is a centralized service that is trying to develop features that are wanted by the most customers. This means that features are driven by marketing reasons and certainly not by any outside group.

Testing in this environment is not so critical. It takes a lot to get even a somewhat stable and adequately functional website built. The estimates for how long it will take to build a website are as bad, if not worse, than those for enterprise systems.

If there are errors they are fixed as quickly as possible and the new code is put up on the website. Any client logging in after that will be using the new code. Because of this fast fix-and-deploy cycle there is a tendency to use the clients as the QA department. No one client is that important, so if a particular client is inconvenienced it isn't a major problem. Hence, testing is easy because there is not as much of it done. Early users of these services have a rough road, so it is essential that the service being offered is compelling enough that clients will put up with it.

The data in these services has to remain valid for an account. If there are major logic changes then the website can shut down and convert the old data to the new requirements.

When you look at the three factors as applied to cloud software:

- Cloud software companies have totally centralized control and they control every decision made about the software.

- They produce some test data to get started but largely they use their clients for testing.

- There is a requirement to keep the old data a client is using operational despite the addition of new features. This does add difficulty to this kind of software.

ENTERPRISE

Finally, we come to Enterprise software where things are much harder.

Once, I was building a system for a large union. I still believed in methodologies, and I had a design document. I wanted to make what the system did and didn't do very clear. There was a feature that was clearly listed, in large type, that the system would *not* have. All the managers signed off on the design. When the system started to be used operationally, one of the staff came to me and said that she couldn't do her job without that feature.

Now what was I to do?

I could have taken a hard stand and said that it wasn't in the deliverables, but an enterprise system is about having a system that works for that particular organization. I had no real choice. If the system couldn't handle the union's operations then it would probably be rejected. I had to add the feature. Clearly, I didn't have total control over features.

The control over change rests mainly with the user base. The enterprise system has to allow people to do their jobs and process information. If a feature is missing it may mean that someone doesn't have the information they need, or that they will have to go through a time-consuming activity to produce it some other way (usually using a spreadsheet).

Then there are changes. If there is a tax change introduced by a level of government, the organization has no choice but to respond to it. If senior management mandates some organizational change, the system will have to respond. Changes happen all the time in enterprises and they require changes in systems to support the new ways of doing things.

The Phoenix payroll system has been installed for over three years, and there have been several union contracts with the federal government renegotiated in that time. This throws a whole lot of extra programming into the already overstretched project team.

Just think of a system like the Phoenix payroll system. How do you test this? In the scientific/engineering software and packaged software they tested on sample after sample. Those samples contained all the variations to test most code paths. In a word processor, the code paths are the same for typing "Lorem ipsum" as "Dear Friend," it's only the data that is different. In the case of cloud software, they largely use the users for testing. There can be bugs that make the cloud software unusable for a small group of clients. It's tough on those clients but not a killer for the cloud software company. However, in enterprise software there is only one client and the software has to work for it. Any bug that stops operations is a red-light-flashing and siren-screaming emergency.

In a system like payroll software, you have to have test cases that cover a good percentage of the possibilities. Think of all the possibilities that a person working under a union contract could generate. Given all the combinations and permutations of working (statutory holidays, more than eight hours in a day, shifts after midnight, lunch breaks, booked salary leaves, garnishees), it is clear that to do a proper test you need far, far more test data than actually exists. These employees individually fit into an incredibly tiny percentage of the possible situations, but any of those huge number of combinations are possible at any time and are required to work flawlessly.

There are always lots of bugs that appear when you start to use a system in a real organization. These bugs don't come up in QA testing. In the case of a payroll system you might have actual or historical data for a few hundred employees under a union contract, which will only test a small fraction of the possible conditions.

To make things worse, the contracts change periodically as they are renegotiated. There is no way you can generate the test data to really certify this software. When it comes to delivering stable software, you have to test. As we have seen, in all other kinds of software they test and test and test, until there is a version that passes all that testing and all the known bugs are acceptable.

But enterprise software is much harder. Basically, the only way is to do your testing in the guise of installation. What is usually being installed is the package world's idea of beta software, at best. All you can do is some simple testing, and then turn it loose on real life and fix it when it goes wrong. The reality is that a lot of what is installed is not feature complete. Often some features, such as reports that aren't needed right away, can wait for a delayed implementation.

You can see that in all the other software types the objectives were specified. When I was writing software to help determine the exact direction a radar antenna was pointing, it was clear what was wanted. We wanted the most accurate angle that we could extract from the data, because that increased the quality of the image.

That never changed throughout the project.

If you are working on some packaged software there is a set of features to implement. In reality some of those features are dropped and some new ones may be added during the build. But it is the team that really determines that. It is the software manufacturer that determines what features are to be included and what ones are not. It is the software manufacturer that determines how that feature will be implemented and it does that with input from marketing, who think they understand what users want, and development, who want to do things in ways that are easier to implement.

In enterprise computing what is needed is much less clear. It resides in the minds of the operational staff, who aren't systems people and often don't remember something they need until later when they have to perform some task.

So, what is being built is not totally clear, and the builders don't have control over what is wanted; that power is spread out in the organization.

This is very difficult to control. On top of this, the business logic can change month to month. This can be the result of some environmental change, such as government regulations, or it can be because of organizational reorganization, or policy changes, or contract renegotiations.

Consequently, the project team has to deal with constant changes. This doesn't happen in aerospace programming—the speed of light doesn't change, Saturn doesn't suddenly decide to go around the sun in the opposite direction.

But you can get changes in the organization world that, because of NLP, can have totally unanticipated and serious consequences.

In enterprise computing the organization's operational needs dictate the features. As an IT person you can complain all you like, but when the user says "I can't do my job without that feature" you are kind of up against the wall.

In enterprise, unlike other kinds of software, you are trying to build new software, not knowing what features you may be required to implement during the project. If the project takes longer than you have estimated (surely that never happens!), then the number of new features inevitably goes up, because all organizations change over time.

When you look at the three factors as applied to enterprise software, you can see how they add to the difficulty of these systems:

- Enterprise systems are trying to home in on what works for the organization. The features needed are not really known until the system is used.

- Testing is really difficult and is usually mostly done by the users when they start to use the system. Once an organization has switched to a new system everything is an emergency. But that means that design is ongoing and if there is already a large amount of entropy these problems could put it over the edge.

- Business rules change from period to period. However, all the old data has to be kept operational as it is combined with new data to produce business reports. This results in a complexity that just isn't there in other kinds of software. It is like fixing an airplane while in flight.

SUMMARY

Enterprise systems have some properties that other software simply doesn't have. Control over features doesn't reside solely with the project team; the team is at the mercy of people in the organization who are trying to communicate what they need but don't always know what that is until later. Testing is often done on the live system. Once the system is running, the code has to be able to respond to changes in the business logic, and yet keep all the past results.

As a programmer, it is much easier to work on other kinds of software. Trying to develop software while keeping it in sync with the activities of a growing and changing organization is really, really hard.

Let us now turn our attention to fallacies of enterprise systems. These are commonly-held beliefs that arise out of our physical world common sense and lead us astray when making decisions about enterprise computers.

11

FOUR FALLACIES OF
ENTERPRISE SYSTEMS

FALLACY #1: IT'S EASIER TO CHANGE AN EXISTING PROGRAM THAN TO WRITE A NEW ONE

From the 1960s through the 1980s it was becoming more and more apparent that implementing enterprise systems was incredibly prone to failure, and even "successful" software was often unreliable, inefficient, and hard to use. Starting in the 1990s software manufacturers decided to offer systems that could be "customized" or "configured" to produce a system that met the needs of the client.

This is physical world way of thinking, because in the physical world if you have a machine that does something close to what you want, it is usually easy to modify it to do the task you want done. This is a consequence of the locality of effect in physical systems.

Suppose you have a physical project in the desert and require a fleet of trucks. You can get a good deal for a fleet of trucks that were used in the north. The trucks are fine except that they have heaters and not air conditioners. It seems pretty straightforward to replace the heaters with air conditioners. This feeling is a result of our common sense about effects being local in physical systems. The heaters take up space, use power and add weight to the truck. Air conditioners use those resources as well. If we can get an air conditioner unit that draws about the same amount of power as the heater, and can fit into the same space, then we are good. Heaters and air conditioners are going to be roughly the same weight for a given size, so the air conditioner will most likely have minimal impact on the overall weight of the truck.

All of these considerations are local to the part of the truck where the heaters were. As long as the air conditioner doesn't take excessive resources, in terms of power, weight, and size, it will be fine to replace the heater. All of those issues can be checked ahead of time by examining the specifications on the air conditioner units.

This concept of having a solution close to what you want and modifying it to fit the need is so compelling that it seems obvious. If you have need for a payroll system, and a software company has a payroll system being used by one of their clients, it just seems to make sense that it is easier to take that already-existing payroll system and modify it to fit the needs of your company.

When you think of this, you probably think of all the payroll calculations that are done in a payroll system; the screens that get payroll information, and the logic to write checks. "Surely," you might be thinking, "all that is the same. It must save work not to have to write that." Remember, though, that the software world is not the same as the physical world. In the software world, all the specific logic of setting up a system for one particular company may get in the way and lessen the chances of success.

Programmers have to go into all that code and try to modify it to fit the new client. If the code is high entropy, it is impossible for a human to map out all the impacts of code changes on the rest of the system. When programmers modify software to try to repurpose it, there is a distinct risk that these changes will cause serious problems throughout all the code and fixing those problems may cause even more problems.

As we will see later in this book, this may lead to a "system death spiral" where errors cause even more errors, and it becomes beyond the capability of the team to bring the system to stability.

SOMETIMES IT'S JUST NOT WORTH RENOVATING

In the 1990s I was running a contract software house that was providing programming services to large software companies like Microsoft and Adobe. When we reached around 30 employees we were running out of space. We were renting part of the top floor of a nice building, but we were concerned about the cost of increasing that space. We considered buying a building. The realtors showed us several properties. One was a large building that had previously been used by a garment company. The price was good. There was far more space than we needed, but we could sublet the extra space, which would give us options as we grew in the future.

However, the building was old. I had an electrician report on the power and it wasn't good. It was going to take a lot of work to bring it all up to the level we needed to safely run all of our computer equipment. There was no air conditioning, which was common in older buildings in Vancouver, but with every employee running at least one computer, and some of them running several computers, we would need air conditioning. All in all, I concluded that this building was just not going to be adapted easily to our company.

But all of these issues were visible and independent of each other. If there is just one issue it is much easier to see that a building might work for a company. Say the plumbing is an issue. The rest of the infrastructure is fine, but the plumbing is substandard. You can get an estimate to see the cost of fixing the plumbing. And if you totally replace it, it should give you no problems as it will all be brand-new, freshly-installed work. In the physical world we take that as an indication of quality. Real estate agents routinely boast about recently updated electrical and plumbing systems.

The plumbing won't impact the electrical. If the electrical is fine then it can be kept as is. This locality gives an independence of variables between different areas and allows us to accurately weigh the cost of decisions.

Also, most of these things are relatively obvious. We can all look at plumbing and get a good impression of whether it is modern and up to standard or whether it is antiquated and patched together. We can certainly hire a plumber who can look at it and give an expert opinion.

However, in software, nothing is obvious. Software is invisible, silent. There are hundreds of thousands, maybe even millions of lines of code. If you are not a professional software developer it is incomprehensible to you. Even if you are an experienced software developer it is hard to assess how well the code is written. You can't examine all the code, and there may be whole areas written by someone who had a questionable grasp of software development and has introduced high-entropy code that is an accident waiting to happen.

This is a really hard thing to come to grips with. It just seems so sensible to take an existing system and modify it. Surely it is easier? Non-programming managers just cannot believe that building a system from scratch could be easier than modifying a system with similar functionality.

It is so obvious that it is rarely questioned.

This has been the single biggest trap in the whole history of enterprise computing.

"This application is similar so let's just modify it."

"Surely it's easier to have a working system to start from."

The software equivalent to an old tired building with leaks and an elevator that breaks down regularly is entropy. But unlike the defects of an old building, software entropy is invisible to most managers. Unless you understand systems and the various languages that make up their components, it is hard to detect entropy. Code gets old. If it has been changed many times to accommodate new features, has had a variety of coding styles over the years and different programmers of varying abilities working on it, it can be as cranky and as trouble-prone as that old elevator that keeps trapping people between floors.

There is also a feeling that the people who wrote the original software have an expertise that the developers modifying the software don't have. This is a belief that somehow modifying working software is easier than developing it in the first place. After all, the structures are there, "all they have to do" is make some changes to accommodate the new application. This is an echo of the designer/builder paradigm that is so prevalent in the physical world. The programmers who built the system are somehow regarded as more accomplished than those who maintain it. Maintenance engineer is not a high-status title in the software world.

Whenever someone says "all you have to do" in relation to software, then you should be very afraid. It is a phrase I have heard countless times in my software career, and it always seems to be the prelude to a knotty, difficult problem that can have very bad outcomes.

This is another instance of our physical common sense not being applicable to a software situation. If we have a truck with a flatbed and we want it to transport liquids, it is much easier to take off the flat bed and install a tank than it is to start from scratch and build a new truck. Weight is weight, and if a truck can handle five tons of rock on the flatbed, it is reasonable to expect it to have no trouble with a tank that weighs five tons when full.

That is another application of our sense of locality of effect. The effect of a truck load is the force imposed on the frame, axles and wheels. As long as we keep a load somewhat similar, then the engine and drive train should not really be impacted. We clearly don't want to open up the massive problem of designing a whole new engine and drive train, and there is no reason to do that. However, a seemingly analogous situation in software has no such ability to guarantee that whole parts of the system can remain unchanged. NLP can easily cause changes to sweep through the system, forcing rewrites of seemingly disconnected areas.

Having to transition from an existing situation to a new one can be far more difficult than just writing the new situation in the first place.

ENTROPY IN THE SOURCE CODE

As soon as you start changing a system's code you have taken working software and turned it into a hunk of untested code. You are now in a battle with entropy. What results is the project team fighting a desperate fight, trying to find a stable, low-entropy spot to settle on, and not let the entropy beast turn things into an uncontrollable, non-performing confusion.

Entropy sets many traps for the unwary, less experienced programmer. Why not try a short, fast dash—slap in the changes as quick and dirty as we can and get out of here? I've seen people adopt that strategy and then still be trying to claw their way out of the mess two years later.

One complication in all this confusion is that it sometimes works. If the existing system is close enough, i.e. there are no fundamental architectural differences, then it may be possible to modify the software reasonably quickly. So sometimes an enterprise software project will more or less succeed. The trick is figuring out if you have software that can be modified or if you have something that is intrinsically incompatible with what you want to achieve.

Let's look at a hypothetical example. Take a payroll system. To the unwary, one payroll system is like another. You see a payroll system that is working for several companies and you decide to use it. After all, it's a working payroll system, it pays people correctly and on time, and you need a payroll system. *All you have to do* is modify the working system to fit your needs. Sounds logical, doesn't it?

But to the programmer, things are not so easy. Let's suppose that the working system is used for international companies and consolidates results. Our new system is for a government that has many bargaining units with different contracts, i.e. different payroll calculations. I'll call any pay arrangement with a group of employees a bargaining unit, whether it's an actual union contract or a group of salaried employees, all of whom negotiate their compensation individually.

The original system treats the different national companies as independent bargaining units, each with its own employees and payroll calculations. For example, the French company has different laws, different deductions, and different overtime policies than the U.S. one, which has its own employees and payroll policies.

However, let's say a government customer wants the same people to work in different bargaining units. They may have someone being paid under two different programs, or someone may work for the government in a different role, working on an election or doing some hourly data collection work on a research project. The government wants all of that to be combined and the employee given one deposit and one pay stub.

This kind of situation occurs all the time in these modification efforts. It's a change of hierarchy. In the working system the hierarchy is companies (i.e. bargaining units) having a one-to-many relationship to employees (i.e. each bargaining unit has many employees). In the modified system we have employees having a one-to-many relationship with bargaining units (i.e. each employee having one or more bargaining units). We still have each bargaining unit having many employees, so it is a much more complicated relationship tree.

Now the manager is saying, "Hey, it's just a payroll system, and the new client wants a payroll system. How hard can it be?"

It can be really, really hard.

Inverting hierarchies is a major change to a system. All through the code base there have been assumptions made about the relationship between employees and bargaining units. There is no concept of combining pay results from one bargaining unit with another. Each one is treated independently. They may have different payroll runs, one paying monthly the other bi-weekly. This wasn't a problem before because they were independent from each other.

Now you come to make this change. All those assumptions, that run throughout hundreds or thousands of lines of code are no longer true. Now the business logic has to start with employees and descend to bargaining units.

There are screens and reports that start at the bargaining unit and work down to the employees. Whoops.

Now you have to travel from employee to the bargaining units. The database has to be changed. In the old system you had a bargaining unit stored for each employee, and for each employee you could get the bargaining unit data and work with it. Now, however, there are multiple bargaining units for an employee. Instead of one bargaining unit, you now have to get a list of bargaining units and process them.

These are extensive changes. There are major hacks to the screens, reports, database, and the payroll computations. The assumption of one bargaining unit per employee has been relied upon in subtle ways throughout the entire codebase. Some of them are obvious and can be changed quickly; a lot more are subtle dependencies that you will only find with testing and using a debugger.

If this code base already has high entropy then these changes will be challenging to say the least. There are always dormant bugs in a system: bugs that don't cause any actual problems. This is especially true of high-entropy code. If the code has been hacked and changed then there could be thousands and thousands of these dormant defects. Making a change like this is going to trigger a lot of them to suddenly have impacts. This is on top of all the bugs that are being introduced by changing the code. All that disorder of badly worded or missing comments, badly labeled methods, duplicated code that can get out of step, existing bugs, and a host of other high disorder properties will come back to bite the poor programmers struggling to get the system working for the new organization.

In that case, it would have been far better to start over and write a custom approach. There are all kinds of libraries and utilities that can handle tasks like check printing and screen formatting. So there really isn't a lot of value in many of those features that we think of when we think of an abstract concept like a "payroll system".

This just illustrates that in the software world, changing an existing system is not as easy a job as modifying equipment is in the physical world. It is like stepping out in the dark from a tent perched on a small summit with steep sides. You fumble around hoping to find the place you want, not knowing if the next step will send you hurtling down into a rocky valley below.

This misconception is probably the single biggest cause of enterprise system failure when you look at it in the light of NLP and entropy. All of the major ERP systems depend on "customizing" the software. It would seem from all the industry surveys over the last 30 years that this works at most 50% of the time.

The response to this has been interesting. All kinds of consultants advise you to keep customization down to a minimum. They point out that it is safer to change your organization's procedures to fit the software rather than change the software to fit the organization. This totally depresses me. The idea that the tail (software) would wag the dog (organization) in this manner is just crazy. Businesses should have the software that fits their needs exactly, and not have to modify their procedures because of the brittle nature of available software that makes it dangerous to do anything more than minor modifications.

FALLACY #2: COMPLEX CODE IS MORE VALUABLE THAN SIMPLE CODE

The Large Hadron Collider (LHC) takes up a circle 27km in circumference. It is buried 50 to 175 meters in the ground and is partly in Switzerland and partly in France. It uses enough power to heat 300,000 homes.

Particles are accelerated around the 27km pipe, in which all the air has been pumped out to form a near perfect vacuum. All around the circumference are power-hungry radio wave generators that pulse out waves that boost the particles as they go by. Particles are also accelerated in opposite directions and then steered into over a billion head-on collisions a second. The resulting shower of particles is detected by arrays of incredibly sensitive instruments and processed with thousands of computers. Probing the nature of reality on the scale of sub-atomic particles is a problem of mind-boggling complexity. The solution is the LHC, the most complicated machine humankind has ever built.

There is no doubt that a complex problem requires a complex solution. The flip side of this is that we naturally assume the inverse: if a solution is complicated then the problem it solves must be complicated, too.

And that is generally true in the physical world. In fact, we find Rube Goldberg machines a source of amusement. We laugh because of the ridiculous mismatch between the complexity of the machine and the simplicity of the task being accomplished. Our physical common sense tells us that no one would go to all the trouble to build a complex machine when a simpler one would suffice.

But software is different.

Unnecessary complexity is one of the many forms of software entropy. In software, complexity comes as a default. Code that is being hacked on by an ever-changing staff will get more complex. Code that is no longer used will be left in, and code will be duplicated because one programmer will not know that another programmer has implemented essentially the same thing. Features get added and then not removed as no one knows if anyone uses them or not. Programmers in a rush don't comment their code, or they comment it but forget to change the comment when the code changes. Programmers name functions with misleading names.

145

Complexity in software is the default. Bad code is more complex than good code. In most huge software systems there is a simpler algorithm struggling to be seen.

When companies brag about the millions of lines of code they have, they are using people's tendency to think that this is a massive technical effort that only a big company could pull off, and it must be an incredibly hard problem. In reality, it may be a lot simpler problem, and the scale of their software is more a reflection of the buildup of entropy than cutting-edge engineering.

You can take it from me, having worked on MS Office code bases, that any software that has been through many releases with hundreds of programmers of various abilities and experience working on it for various amounts of time, has high entropy.

ENTROPY IN THE SOURCE CODE

Say you have two watches, one just tells the time, the other has an additional display that tells phase of the moon. Which one is more expensive? Well the second one, obviously. We are used to dealing with physical objects in that manner. The car costs $30,000 but if you want the sun roof that will be an extra $1,000.

Why do we expect to pay for extra stuff?

Well, obviously, to install a sun roof requires extra costs. There is a motor and controls plus the track and rollers that let the sun roof move back and forth. Of course it costs extra money.

There is also a tendency in physical products towards simplicity to reduce costs. If a machine has a set of four gears that can be replaced by one, the manufacture will try to do that. It probably costs around four times as much to buy four gears as it does to buy one, so in this way the manufacture can reduce manufacturing costs and the savings can be kept as profit or passed on to the customers. Such a reduction may also reduce weight and increase reliability.

Software is different. In software complexity costs nothing, in fact, as we have seen, complexity is the default. If you work on a code base and don't have a clear picture of exactly what you are trying to achieve globally, and how each small component fits into that design, then the result of changes will inevitably be increased complexity, which means increased entropy.

Complexity in software is bad, and it is the default. There isn't an acquisition cost as there is for complexity in physical systems. You get it for free. It takes careful thinking to come up with the simplest program. Programs done in a rush are always overly complicated.

Bloated software requires bloated fixes. One example is when the same logic is implemented many times in a system. This violates the DRY (Don't Repeat Yourself) principle of software engineering, which mandates that this code be in only one place and be executed when needed.

How does this happen? Maybe a developer didn't notice that someone else had already created that function. If it's buried in various modules it just might not be noticed that it should be made common. If a situation arises where that code needs to be modified, it will have to be modified in all the places it was duplicated. Each duplication was a separate implementation, so they are all somewhat different, with different names and different approaches. So, the change has to be figured out separately for each place it was duplicated.

All software moves toward increased complexity. As you add features the number of lines of code grows, which means more complexity. As you fix bugs you add handling for cases that weren't foreseen, and again, the software grows in complexity. It's a continual fight to try to keep the code simple and straightforward, given all these changes. I am delighted when I can remove a few hundred lines of code and replace it with something much simpler.

This makes software systems a uniquely difficult environment, with the characteristic that if you don't expend a huge and constant amount of effort on controlling the beast it will grow and grow, and if never checked the software will eventually become un-maintainable.

This means that when a manufacturer says that they have millions of lines of code in their product, you should not think that is a sign of significant engineering, you should think of it as a sign of a bloated codebase.

FALLACY #3: UNUSED FEATURES HAVE NO IMPACT

A few years ago, I visited a distributor of specialty wood processing equipment on Annacis Island, an industrial area on the outskirts of Vancouver. They were using an ERP package from one of the big vendors. As is common, they had had a lot of problems customizing it. It had taken a long time, and there were still some strange postings appearing in the inventory account that they had to reverse out each month. When I visited, the system had been operational for about a year.

The accountant showed me the input screen they were using to enter their sales orders. It had a large number of controls at the top: buttons, drop downs, and menu choices. The screen itself was like a closely-packed spreadsheet with a lot of columns that could hold entered data. I remarked on the number of columns. He laughed and started scrolling horizontally. My mouth dropped open as the columns went on and on. I looked at these columns, all of which had complicated descriptions, and asked what they were for. He shrugged, and said he had no idea. They didn't use all of those columns. To enter a sales order, they had to enter certain columns and avoid the rest. As far as all those controls on the top of the form were concerned, the accountant had no idea what most of them did. They were all features he didn't use and had no interest in.

He then told me about a summer intern who was entering in sales orders. She got confused by the column names and entered data into some of the unused ones. This caused the software to put an unexpected record into their database. Because that caused an error every time it was read from the database, it crashed the entire system immediately on startup. It took a week of being shut down to clean it all up, because the program they were using to clean the database was out of date, and when they ran it, all the records in the database were erased. They went to a backup, but the only one they had was a month old. They re-entered all the data for the last month, which was a lot because this was just after a major trade show, and there was a flood of orders resulting from the show. Fixing the maintenance program and debugging it, and then running it on the database, took three weeks. It took a month to catch up with the backlog of orders, and then they had to deal with a massive problem because without a system to monitor committed resources they had hand-written too many orders, requiring equipment modifications, and didn't have the staff to complete them on time.[19]

Bottom line; unused features cost you money.

They are a form of entropy. A feature that is there, that you don't use, or doesn't do anything useful for your operations, is an accident waiting to happen. There is always the chance that someone will use them acci-

---

[19] You can see the entropy of having out-of-date utility programs and not keeping a really up-to-date backup combines with the original problem to produce a cascade of issues all of which throw the system into states that are more and more unusual which in turn can uncover bugs that have never been encountered before. Entropy is like a frantic horse; once it is out in the yard bucking and kicking and generally creating chaos; it is hard to get back into the barn.

dentally and take your system into states that the programmers didn't take into account. Couple that with NLP and you can see where that leads.

If you don't have that button or menu choice in your system then it is impossible for someone to accidentally use it, and none of those possible bad things can happen. You will have lower entropy.

I have had people say that the manufacturer is throwing features in for free—as if that were a benefit. This is a physical world way of thinking of things. Those features are not free, they are entropy, and they interfere with your operations and cost you money.

One has to ask "Why is it in a system?" That is a good question. There is no reason for a system to have unused features—they are there because the vendor is trying to make their system work for as many clients as possible and whoever customized the software was too lazy to remove them.

There is not only the danger of using features that don't apply to your particular case. There is also the visual clutter of extra features. This makes the interface more confusing, and hence increases the probability of human error when operating the system.

This is all done for the benefit of software manufacturers rather than the customer. It is all about the needs of the marketing department. If they can say they have a feature that even a small part of the market finds useful, then they can increase the target market. This is the software manufacturer's agenda, not yours. They get to advertise all those capabilities, which all sound good, but their customers will suffer increased entropy from unused features, which will translate into increased costs, if not outright disaster.

There should be a law of enterprise system design "All operations available to a user *must* do something essential to the data processing of the company."

This would mean there are no unused features or even any controls, like a button, a menu choice, or a tab that do nothing useful. It would mean there are no entry fields that don't apply to that organization. Anything less than that is just giving entropy a chance to come in and spread disorder.

This is, of course, against the financial interests of companies selling ERP software. They keep adding as many features as possible to continually try to increase their target markets. At the same time, they can point to the software, with its incredibly complicated interface and charge more money for it because it is complicated, which in the physical world means valuable.

But it costs you, the customer, money. There is more chance for mistakes and it greatly complicates customization. If you go into the code and start changing things there is a chance that what you disrupt is some unused feature. But if you never test it because it shouldn't be used, some error is waiting for the poor unwary operator who accidentally chooses that menu choice.

That is the kind of seemingly random behavior that makes people think there is a ghost in the machine. Someone gets into an unused form and then clicks on the wrong thing and it crashes. There's a good chance they won't remember exactly what was going on at the time, and it just becomes another one of those unexplained occurences. In the worst case this crash causes some data corruption that takes a major effort, hence cost, to correct.

So, avoid unused features. Tell your vendor to remove them. They are costing you money. This is part of what you have to know when selecting software, and we shall look at this in more detail later when talking about how to push back on software salespeople.

FALLACY #4: LARGE COMPANIES ARE MORE COMPETENT IN ENTERPRISE SOFTWARE THAN SMALLER COMPANIES

No doubt when the Phoenix payroll system was sold the government representatives were very impressed by the fact that IBM was the contractor. After all, IBM is an international company whose very name echoes with decades of being at the forefront of computer research.

In the physical world this kind of reputation is a reliable way of qualifying contractors. People just assume that large, profitable companies are extremely competent at what they do. Largely that is true. Normally the reason they got to be large and profitable is that they do something better than other companies. They develop expertise and in-house systems that allow them to manufacture complicated devices efficiently.

When we think of General Electric we think of their amazing manufacturing expertise in producing reliable, high-powered jet engines. They exemplify competence.

You wouldn't buy a jet engine from a machine shop down the street. We expect that complicated, expensive technology like a jet engine has to come from a major corporation that has a track record in building them and has a major research and development process to continually improve them.

But what does GE bring to the manufacturing of jet engines that makes it possible for them, but hard for someone small trying to break into the business? Let's take the example of a turbine blade, just one part of the thousands that make up a jet engine. GE has designed its shape using mathematics, computer simulations, and air tunnels. That's a huge amount of work to determine the optimal shape and composition. They have to find a manufacturer who can work with that kind of steel or carbon fiber precisely enough. They have to have machines to measure it to check whether it meets specs.

All of this is a huge amount of corporate knowledge. To set this up from scratch is daunting. And this is just one small part of an engine, so this vast amount of effort to capture expertise is repeated thousands of times across many other areas. It's a massive effort that requires a large organization to co-ordinate.

When that turbine blade is designed it is designed in a 3D CAD program. Automated tools can machine small-scale prototypes or full-scale examples using the design. If GE decides to try a new alloy it can be machined and then tested. Physical properties are easy to identify and quantify. There is the weight, strength, shape, and performance. They can all be quantified and tested.

But software is different.

Remember software's lack of proportionality of effect. Maintenance can be as destabilizing as major architecture changes. There is no direct way to transform designs into code. We have seen how it is impossible to separate out the design phase from the build phase in software, and how hard it is to build enterprise systems. We have also seen that building software is a uniquely human activity.

So, what does a company like IBM bring to the production of enterprise software? They don't have special software tools or techniques that others don't have. They have some proprietary computer languages, but no one believes they are better in any way than the languages used commonly in the industry. For example, the Phoenix system is written in a language called PeopleCode a language owned by Oracle. PeopleCode is just another computer language. Like all computer languages it has some better and some worse features, but nothing that makes any real difference to development. Using a proprietary language also has a disadvantage in that there is a much smaller pool of programmers to draw from, and many good programmers don't want to invest the time to come up to speed on it. There is so much software available, either free or under license, that no one has a lock on some propriety solution that is considerably better than anyone else. IBM may have propriety enterprise software that is not available to others, but it is just software similar to thousands of other alternatives of similar capability.

In enterprise software there are no parts where you can accumulate expertise in their design and manufacturing. Parts in software, if they have any analogy to components in physical devices, are supplied in the software libraries as basic functionality like: handling lists, sorting, scaling images, and interfacing with the file system. Equivalent libraries are available to everyone, and large organizations have no special knowledge about them, or unique expertise in using them.

The one thing that large software companies try to make into an advantage is their enterprise software that can be customized. These are large, complex codebases that have many modules to handle various common business functions like inventory, accounts payable, accounts receivable and general ledger. However, we have seen that it is a fallacy to believe that you get huge value out by starting with existing software. The Phoenix payroll system is certainly an example of starting with an existing system going horribly wrong.

The software world is just different and there is no real in-house expertise for large companies that make it impossible for small organizations to compete. In fact, as we shall see, smaller organizations are usually a better choice.

STAFF

If the software tools and techniques are not special, what about the people? Does a large organization have some

HR advantage that allows them to recruit better people, train them better, and cause them to create better software by active supervision?

There is, as in all industries, a status hierarchy in the software industry. Most of the best people are drawn away by the siren call of cool technologies. This is not enterprise computing. So that leaves enterprise computing selecting from a pool whose average talent is below the average of programmers as a whole.

While there are some really good people who work for large software vendors, the rank and file are certainly no better than any other enterprise computing shop. I have hired, worked with, and known hundreds of programmers in my career. Of the ones who worked in enterprise software some went on to work for large software companies and some moved to smaller regional or local organizations. My anecdotal experience (certainly not a scientific survey) is that the good programmers split fairly evenly between large and small companies, but most of the less-talented programmers ended up in the larger organizations. My belief is that this is because in those large companies career advancement is not so connected to programming ability.

MOST ERP CODE WAS WRITTEN BY SMALL COMPANIES

The irony is that almost all the ERP software offered by large software companies was developed by small software companies.

In the late 1980s and 1990s it was small companies like Great Plains Software in Fargo, North Dakota that started doing multi-user enterprise systems on PCs. A single individual, Doug Burgum, wrote the software marketed by Great Plains Software when it was just a small company scrambling for clients. There were other companies like NavVision and Axapta, as well as PeopleSoft.

The problem for these small companies was that the development environments on PCs at that point were not really good enough for even middle-sized business systems. Consequently, they mostly invented their own languages that had in them features they needed that are now common in all popular languages.

In the early 2000s the large companies woke up to the fact that they could buy large groups of customers by buying these companies that had been successful during the 1990s. Oracle bought PeopleSoft. Microsoft bought five separate companies: Great Plains, Solomon, Axapta, Navvision, and Concorde. Microsoft tried to integrate them but the project failed. So, Microsoft did with marketing what they couldn't do with software. They merged them all under the Microsoft Dynamics label, giving each a two-letter qualifier. For example, Microsoft Dynamics-NV and Microsoft Dynamics-GP.

It is interesting that each of those is written in a different, totally-proprietary computer language that no other company or software uses. Supporting a computer language for this one-off software product is a strange state to be in for a software manufacturer. However, when you buy a company with a large customer base you are locked in to continuing with that language unless you can migrate them to something else. Microsoft tried to develop a migration strategy but failed, so they are left with these islands of clients that they are trying to rationalize after the fact.

This forces them to support these different computer languages and to provide training for developers who want to customize their software. It also allows developers to charge a lot once they have gained a degree of experience with these unusual languages. One side effect of this is that it increases costs for clients.

Programmers are like everyone else, and they will work in certain circumstances if they are paid extra.

These specialty languages confine a developer to a very small market, and as a rule the languages are unpleasant to work with. For a programmer, unpleasant means simple things take a lot of work, the language is awkward, and bugs are hard to find. By and large, you can tell the most difficult and unlikable environments by the amount that developers charge for working on it. Certain ERP systems command a significant premium over work done on competing software. This is a reflection of what kind of incentive is needed to get programmers to work in that software environment. It can also be used as an indication of what software to avoid.

12
RELATIONAL DATABASE ENTROPY

As far as awkward tools go, relational databases are one of the major contributors to software project entropy. As you will see, the relational database is such an awkward, inefficient, and insecure technology, and yet so ubiquitous, that it is one of the major sources of project entropy.

It deserves a special look as it is interesting to see how bad technologies can become ubiquitous.

In the 1970s a new type of database was proposed by Dr. Codd and Dr. Date of IBM. It was called a "relational" database. Now, I have never seen any indication that either Dr. Codd or Dr. Date ever built a real-life enterprise system. If they had, I think they would have realized that relational calculus was just not a good fit for enterprise systems. Not having to actually make a system work, all they had to do was give highly-contrived academic examples. Anyone who had worked in the trenches of enterprise systems knew that real life was far more complicated. It's just tough to write enterprise software. It is an intersection of computer and human behavior and it is really difficult to get things that satisfy those sometimes conflicting needs.

I was working on software systems for a large union at the time, and I remember everyone was talking about relational databases. It wasn't that any of them really knew what a relational database was, but they had heard the term and it sounded good. It was at a time when computer terms were starting to come into common business parlance. There were a lot of magazines like *Byte* and *PC Mag* starting to appear on newsstands, and some of the stories were being carried in the newspapers. The idea of a database was an appealing one; the idea of something that stored the data like a filing cabinet. It is such a physical world concept that it became something that people who really didn't know much about it started talking about.

Then there was the name, "relational." There were stories about how it would allow you to "travel relationships" throughout your data. Get the name of the department of the project manager of the project, that kind of thing. But actually, the word relation in relational refers to the *mathematical* concept of a relationship, which is a collection of groups of data. If two things are in a group they are said to be related. In fact, the mathematical theory of relations eschews the concept of a connection between the related objects and defines relationship just as the set of the related things. Any such set is a relationship in the mathematical theory. This is completely removed from our business-centric concept of a relationship, where there has to be some kind of a connection. If you had a group of pairs of objects and someone told you they were related, you would look for some kind of connection. There are puzzles that are set up that way, and we have to hunt for the hidden factor. It's a very human instinct for pattern-seeking. But the theory of mathematical relationships doesn't care. They can be considered a relationship even if they are just paired by chance.

When I was teaching mathematical logic at York University I taught a course in the mathematical theory of relations. Some students just couldn't get away from relationships as having some kind of rule. The abstract concept the theory was based on was something they just couldn't get. When I heard that IBM had come out with a proposal for a database based on relational calculus I was startled. Having by that time written lots of enterprise software, I couldn't see how trying to force things into such a formal and abstract structure was going to be helpful.

In my opinion it was one of the most significant contributors to complexity and system overruns. Let me go through this technology and show you some of its problems.

Have you ever seen an old movie, probably set in the 1920s or 1930s where someone is reading a telegram?

It always went something like: HAVE ELOPED WITH DANNY STOP WILL HONEYMOON IN MADRID STOP GLORIOUSLY HAPPY STOP

They were always like that, with all those STOPs. What was that all about?

To understand, we have to go back to the Boer War, which was a nasty war the British fought at the turn of the 20th century in South Africa. As well as introducing the world to the concept of concentration camps and trench warfare, it was the first war to use wireless telegraphy, so that troops could get orders by telegraph right at the front. War fronts are dirty places, even more so at the turn of the twentieth century, with mud and horse manure being splattered all over. Worried that a mud splatter could be mistaken for a comma or a period that might change the intent of an order, the British War Department mandated that all punctuation should be spelled out, for example, COMMA. For the period they chose the short word STOP, named after "full stop" which is a more British name for a "period."

It became a practice to write out the telegraph code for a period as the word STOP. And when people read them out loud they instinctively read out the word STOP rather than just treating it as a period at the end of the sentence.

"What has that got to do with relational databases?" you might ask. The commands to a relational database are given in actual readable text. This text is in a language called SQL (Structured Query Language). SQL uses punctuation to separate the commands, just as the telegram used the word STOP between sentences. In effect the database gets its commands in a stream of text, like a telegram, with STOP between each command[20].

Look at this example:

> *UPDATE CUSTOMER_TABLE SET NAME="John Smith" WHERE CUSTOM_NO=2333 STOP UPDATE …*

That is a command in SQL to update customer record 2333 setting the name to John Smith.

Now notice the text between the quotes i.e. "John Smith". Where did that come from?

Well it was entered by someone in a browser filling in a form. The person filling in the form typed in "John Smith" and hit the submit button. The web site code put what was typed in between quotes into the SQL statement and sent it to the database for execution.

Now suppose the customer is nefarious and types in this for his name:

> *John" STOP DELETE CUSTOMER_TABLE STOP*

If the web site just puts it into the SQL statement it ends up looking like:

> *UPDATE CUSTOMER_TABLE SET NAME="John" STOP DELETE CUSTOMER_TABLE STOP" STOP UPDATE…*

---

[20] They actually use semicolons and other characters but I'm using STOP in the examples to keep it looking like a telegram.

And perhaps you can see what it has been changed to. There is a command to set a name in the customer table to John, which will be done, but then it will do the next command inserted by the nefarious customer, which is an instruction to delete a whole table of data. Remember that this writing to the database is being done by a task that has to have sufficient rights to update the database.

That is what is called "SQL Injection."

SQL Injection has been the single biggest technique for website hacking and company intrusions. Over 90% of all the major website penetrations were done via SQL injection. You just have to google it and see a flood of data breaches that total into hundreds of millions of credit cards being compromised, bank accounts drained, and personal information exposed.

Pay close attention to what is going on here. The database commands are in text, and the data entered from web forms by Internet users is merged into that text, which allows people filling in the form to try to fool the database into interpreting the command incorrectly.

If this seems to you like a stupid way of doing things you are exactly correct.

This is probably the dumbest technological decision ever to be used extensively by so many, and at so much cost.

This is the software equivalent of a nuclear power plant combining the control room with the visitor's gallery.

It makes no sense to have two things separated, one the commands and the other the data from the forms, then to mix them up, and then to fight a technical back-and-forth battle trying to not get fooled into thinking the data is actually part of the command.

Why mix them up in the first place?[21]

This is just a terrible architecture and it is responsible for billions of dollars in damage to organizations around the world.

But the relational database story gets worse.

Let's say you have a timesheet that you have implemented in software. The timesheet has an employee number. Now you are displaying the time sheet and you want to get the name of the employee. That is on the Employee table, so you have to create an SQL statement like:

> SELECT EMPLOYEE WHERE EMPLOYEE.NUMBER
> EQUALS TIMESHEET.EMPLOYEE_NUMBER

This takes the employee table and matches it up with the timesheet table, and then you pick. What you are really doing here is defining the relationship between the employee and timesheet. You are saying that they are connected via the employee number that is on the time sheet.

Remember that the timesheet form has already been described to the software. You said the field on the ti-

---

[21] Some programmers will protest this. They will say they can send the data separately and avoid this by using a certain specialized feature called "sql parameters." That is true, but this has to be done every time. If you miss just once, then some bot that is going through every form on your site and probing every field for an opportunity for SQL injection will find it. And of course, it doesn't get done properly every time. Some programmers aren't even aware of these more advanced language features. After all like any profession there is a bottom 20% of programmers who know just enough to be dangerous. In the hundreds of thousands of lines of code, if not millions, it is very difficult to keep checking to make sure someone hasn't made a mistake. Then there is the "do it fast to make sure that it works and then I'll come back and do it properly" factor. A lot of the time programmers forget and don't come back and fix it. In millions of lines of code inside one of thousands of files, it just goes unnoticed.

mesheet was the employee number, so basically at this point that relationship was already known to the software. But now you have to go to all the trouble of constructing an SQL statement and sending it to the database for execution, and then getting back a set of table rows from which you pick out the information you need. This is all totally unnecessary! The information that the timesheet was related to an employee had already been communicated to the software. Using a relational database made it necessary to ignore that information and redefine the relationship in a totally different language.

There is a principle in computer science called the DRY principle, which stands for Don't Repeat Yourself. Its primary thrust is to not repeat code for the same calculation. You should write the code only once and call upon it whenever the calculation is needed. However, it also extends to all kinds of ways of removing redundancy. This is a principle of reducing entropy. Software that uses the same code for the same calculation removes the possibility of those two separate implementations getting out of step.

Using SQL to express "relationships" between data that have already been expressed in a different form is a total violation of the DRY principle. Information is precious in software. When it has been captured it should be squeezed for every possible way it can be used. You should never have to re-enter information. You should never have to enter something that could have been derived from what you have previously entered. To do so is to create a real jump in entropy because now you have introduced the possibility of the two versions of this information getting out of step.

Ever since relational databases were proposed, I have been puzzled as to why this seemingly bizarre architecture has been allowed to persist.

This is like having your filing department speaking a foreign tongue so that all instructions have to be written down in this language.

But it's worse. When you store that timesheet in a relational database you have to totally take it apart, with the header information in one table and all the detail lines that assign hours to projects as separate rows in another table. You have to take apart the form and construct the SQL that takes those bits and stores them. Oh yes, and make sure you put sequence numbers on all those detail lines in the timesheet if you want to get be able to get them back in the same order. When you want the form back, you have to write SQL instructions to join the tables together and then you have to pick out all the timesheet information from the returned results and put it together as a form.

Some people have described this as having to take your car apart each evening when you come home, hang up the parts on your garage wall, and in the morning reassemble your car before you drive to work.

All of this takes a lot of extra code to translate between the different worlds of the relational database and the object world of the software. Extra code means the probability of extra errors, i.e. extra entropy.

As if that wasn't bad enough, the data in a relational database is stored in ways more in keeping with a 1980s programming language than with a modern, object-oriented language. All of the data in today's modern, object-oriented languages have to be encoded into these primitive data types.

This is sometimes referred to as the "object-relational impedance mismatch." Seriously? An impedance mismatch between an amplifier and a speaker I can understand, as it refers to a real physical phenomenon. In this context it is just technobabble, which should be replaced with "consequences of a really stupid architecture."

If you want to know why enterprise systems fail so often this is not the whole cause but it is a major one. The necessity of having to duplicate all of this logic in different languages, and in really different ways of representing data, adds a massive amount of entropy to an ERP system.

Take an older code base with a lot of additions and changes by different people over the years, then try to customize it to a new situation, and throw in all this added entropy of a relational database, and you are putting the project seriously at risk.

That said, it is true that relational databases are ubiquitous. So much so that there are programmers who have never really seen any other kind of database and believe that all databases are relational.

Relational databases have been the worst technology to ever poison a field of endeavor. Dumping this huge amount of extra entropy into systems is a major reason why enterprise systems fail so regularly.

So how did this awful technology become so ubiquitous? That is the subject of our next chapter.

13
THE PERFECT STORM

Why would a technology that is so hard to use, so inefficient, and so insecure, become so dominant?

In 1970, after E. F. Codd proposed using the relational calculus of mathematics as a model for a database, it took a considerable time to come up with a software implementation. A relational database is really easy to implement if you don't care about any kind of efficiency or storage issues. After all, it is all described in mathematics as operations between tables. It is easy to do an in-memory implementation. However, it is an incredibly difficult problem to get a relational database working with small amounts of memory and being forced to store most of the data on disk. This was especially true in the 1970s, when memory was so small and expensive, and disk transfer speeds were so slow. It was so difficult that it took years to come up with code that could actually be used in a system.

What happened was one of those perfect storms of effects that propelled the relational database into prominence.

First, there was the name. Most people misinterpreted it and thought that a relational database actually expressed relationships, instead of understanding that a relational database was data expressed as a set of grids, with named columns and rows of data, which contained absolutely *no* true relationship information, but could be manipulated to express any "relationship," whether useful or not. [22]

The name was catchy. People thought, "Yes, organizations run on relationships, and a database should be able to express these." They had no idea of the disconnect between that conception of causal relationships and the abstract concept of mathematical relationships.

Remember, this was a time when computers were just starting to impinge on people's consciousness. Most organizations had mini-computers, and people were starting to use terminals more and more. Hobbyists were playing with personal computers and the press was full of stories. Since so many more people were now involved with computers there was a larger and more accessible technical press. Everyone wants to appear knowledgeable about the latest things, so the term "relational" was bandied around by people who really didn't understand what it was.

There is nothing new in that. Stereo enthusiasts have always used technical terms that a lot of them didn't really understand (e.g. dynamic range, elliptical stylus, and other terms associated with turntable and amplifier systems). But in this case, it established a perception that a relational database was the latest and most powerful technology. After all, it was all based on a mathematical theory, and how could you argue with that?

There were other database architectures at the time. One of those was what is called multi-valued databases, with Pick being the dominant one. It got its description from the fact that a record could store a list of values, rather than, as in a relational database, taking it apart and storing it in a separate table. I have built systems using both kinds of databases and I can definitely say that it was

_____

[22] In a relational database you can express totally useless relationships as easily as useful ones.

far easier and I was more productive with the multi-valued database than with the relational ones. I observed that the clients using the multi-valued kinds of databases tended to be far happier. Changes were easier, and new reports were quick. Reliability was higher.

But it didn't have the buzz that "relational" got. IBM was on the relational bandwagon because it was a theory developed by their researchers, and in those days IBM was the 800-pound gorilla of the computer industry. So, if IBM said it was a good technology, who could argue with that? Other companies saw an opportunity. Databases had always been integrated into the software. Now they could be separate components and charged for separately.

The buzz around the name "relational" had created a market demand not only before there was even a product, but even before anyone really knew whether it could be implemented or not. People were talking about relational databases and software manufacturers were announcing they would be ready soon. The combination of this presold demand and the idea that they could be sold as another component with separate pricing was irresistible. Companies, realizing that this could be very profitable, feverishly started to develop relational databases.

Given the buzz the name was getting, and the whole mythology that was started about it being based on mathematics, made it sound cutting edge and, well—*complicated*—and hence valuable. People "know" that in physical systems, complex means valuable. The more technologically-complicated companies could make their software sound, the more they could charge for it.

This is where the perfect storm got a push to another level. Relational databases were quite complicated code bases because the relational model is very easy to implement in a simple way, but to make it actually work inside the limitations of an actual computer system is a hugely difficult task. This was especially true when working in the computer environments back in the days when even multi-million dollar mainframes had small memories, and disks had very limited storage, with very slow access times[23]. So just to make them work at all they had to write huge amounts of code to try to optimize the operations.

This created the need for millions of lines of source code, produced by a large team. That meant that, based on the amount of code in relational database software, they were complicated, and our physical world common sense says that complicated things are solving complicated problems, and hence are more valuable. The fact that there were much better database architectures that would solve the same problems with much less complexity was not in the zeitgeist of the time. Physical world common sense says that the more complicated product is more valuable, in that value is directly proportional to complexity, even though that doesn't apply to software.

People also forgave relational databases their obvious flaws of lack of speed, and incredible storage inefficiency. Based on the complexity of the software, it was seen as a very hard problem, so that excused a lot of problems, because it is seen as noteworthy when something that complex works at all.

It is a kind of self-reinforcing argument that, in a perverse way, is quite elegant. What it did, however, was to give the push that started the perfect storm.

This perfect storm was the creation of complexity that became a bit of a gold-rush among technology companies. The database as a separate component had not

---

[23] In 1971 an IBM System/360 Model 22 had 1-4 MB of memory (that's mega bytes, 1/1000 of a gigabyte).

really been a factor in the 1960s and early 1970s. Most applications incorporated some off-the-shelf code that wrote and read disk files. The ERP system I wrote for a national engineering company used standard files to store the data, with simple indices for fast lookup.

The relational database was a separate module that was purchased separately, and because it was really complicated it justified a very high price. It was highly profitable.

It should be noted that the textual nature of the interface, which, as we have seen, is a giant security flaw, really came about to make it possible to package these databases as separate modules. A more sophisticated interface that would be more efficient and secure would require a tighter connection between the application software and the database software. That would make it less portable between systems. The marketing need to package a database as a separate product drove the software architecture—unfortunately for world productivity.

Software companies started to realize that there was profit in the concept of modules. They could divide software up into modules and charge extra for each one. This all added to the aura of complexity that, capitalizing on the tendency of people to view complex things as more valuable than simple things, allowed companies to charge even more. Over a few years the costs of enterprise software grew and grew.

I mentioned before the redundancy in the replies from relational databases. Each "result set" typically has header information duplicated in each record.

For example, a timesheet has a top part (header) that has the employee number and the date. The time sheet has a variable length list of lines that have hours worked and the project worked on. To be stored in a relational database all the headers are stored in one table and all the lines with time and project are stored in another. So, when you want the timesheet back the database has to scan the detail lines for all of the time sheets (this can be a very large number) and pick out the ones that belong to the time sheet you want. This returns a list of the detail lines with each one having the header information attached. In other words, if you have 10 time entries on a timesheet, you will get back 10 lines with the time and project info plus the header info, i.e. the employee number, date, etc. So that employee number, etc. is duplicated 10 times. Over slower networks, this large amount of redundant data takes a lot of time to transmit. In the rush to split systems into more components so they could be charged for separately, some companies realized that this redundancy was impacting the speed with which results were coming back over networks, because earlier networks were very slow.

What followed is a lovely example of how to take a consequence of a badly-designed technology and sell a solution for it. The whole redundancy is totally unnecessary. What the program wants is the timesheet, with one copy of the header, not this artificial, overly large set of data that the timesheet can be constructed from. But rather than fixing the base problem, which is that the relational database wasn't very good in networked environments because of this inefficient way of returning data, the software companies decided instead to sell software that would remove and reinsert this redundancy. Specifically, code removed all the extra copies of the header before sending it over the network, and the receiving software put it all back again so that the programmer would receive it as sent. The beauty of this is that companies got to charge money for this software. They gave it a name "middleware." It proved to be much more profitable to sell compensatory software for architectural defects than to actually fix the architecture itself and make it logical and efficient.

Having the database as a separate entity, often on its own server, meant there was a whole authentication issue, so database interface code had to be installed on clients. Then middleware, if used, had to be inserted in between this and the network communication software. This starts to be very complicated. There are all kinds of chances for failures. There are two ends to the middleware that have to be kept in synchronization as far as versions are concerned.

All this complexity generated money. Corporations were willing to pay big money to improve speeds, and to buy database software. More and more, ERP systems were modularized to be monetized. Being split into optional modules makes systems much more complicated. It is amazing how forcing parts to be self-sufficient and not allowing them to expect other modules to be there can produce some bedeviling logical problems for a programmer to solve. But the agendas that drive these decisions are made by software companies, so profit takes precedence over stability for the end user. In fact, instability is also a profit center. You can blame software issues on bad training and sell extra training courses. Extra income comes from consulting fees, maintenance fees, and upgrades.

By the end of the 1980s, the gold rush was in full swing. Money started pouring into the enterprise software industry. Complexity, it turns out, is very profitable.

And so it has remained for the last 30 years. This has caused an injection of entropy into ERP systems that has greatly contributed to the failure rate.

However, there is an underlying irony to all of this. As we shall see in the next chapter, databases are an anomaly that will only exist for a period while our hardware is still in a primitive stage. Future generations will see databases in the same light as we regard buggy whips—useful in the past, but now just a forgotten part of old technology.

14
DATABASE, A TIME-LIMITED TECHNOLOGY

In the executive briefing in Chapter 5 I showed how memory is just a set of switches whose combinations are used to store numbers. Alan Turing showed that all computations could be done from a small set of operations.

But the whole success of computers is that they can do an incredible number of these small operations in a very short time. This means that it is necessary that the data in the computer's memory be accessible in incredibly short times, and that any of these switches can be accessed in the same time as any other. We are talking nanoseconds—billionths of a second. This allows us to build up highly complex operations out of an incredible number of really simple ones, and to do it in a reasonable time.

Unfortunately, to get this speed, the memory technologies we use today are called "volatile." This is the word engineers borrowed from English to express the concept that its contents only remain as long as the power is on.

If you imagine computer memory as a big line of light switches (as we discussed in Chapter 5), imagine that all those switches that are "on" are held in position by the power being on, and when the power is cut, they all flip back to "off." That is volatile memory.

For the opposite of volatile, engineers chose the word "persistent." Persistent memory is any kind of memory that holds its data even when the power is turned off.

For most of the twentieth century we had recorded music, or other content, on magnetic tapes. They kept their information even when the power was off. If you go to a vacation cabin and find an old tape player and some tapes that haven't been used in decades, they will probably still play. The magnetic information lasts for a long time. It is very persistent.

Initially, data was kept on magnetic tape. Those large reels of half-inch tape looked great in movies as they spun this way and then that. The problem was that they were slow. If you wanted to get to data at the end you had to wind through the whole tape.

Tape was replaced by disks. This was the same magnetic coating but instead of having it covering a long plastic tape, it covered the surface of a spinning disk. Think of the read/write head moving in and out like the arm on a vinyl record; it can read the data as the disk spins below it. Reading data requires the head to move (called seek) to the track it wants to read or write which takes around 5/1000 of a second (5ms). Then there is a wait until the information spins around to come under the head (called latency). Nowadays disks tend to spin at 7200rpm, that is just over 8/1000 of a second (8 milliseconds or 8ms) for one turn. That means, on average, it takes 4ms for the data you want to come under the head. So, to find a piece of data you have to move the head to the right position and wait for it to rotate beneath—this is around 9 milliseconds. Note that all these times are measured in milliseconds, which is a million times slower than the nanoseconds that main memory takes to get to data.

This means that you can't treat disk memory the same as the main computer memory. It is too slow to handle random access to any part of its data—you have to prepare data to be packaged in blocks to write to the disk, and to read you have to read fixed-sized chunks of data at a time and restructure it for main memory.

This problem, that the main memory of a computer (all those switches) is volatile, has bedeviled my career and that of most programmers. Whenever I am storing any kind of data I have to move it to a persistent store. If I don't, it will be lost if the power fails. To do this I have to convert it into a group of bytes that I can write as a block to the disk.

Having to deal with block-structured persistent memory adds a considerable amount of entropy into a computer system. It consumes a lot of code, and it is the source of a lot of problems. When you add incredibly awkward relational databases as a way of persisting data, it becomes a giant amount of entropy.

The irony of all this trouble caused by block storage devices and databases is that it is a detail of systems that will disappear as soon as hardware technology advances.

The breakthrough in computers that will make a huge difference to the success rate of enterprise systems will be high-speed persistent memory. If we had fast computer memory that was not volatile, that kept its data between power shutdowns, then we would not need a database. We would just keep the data in the convenient format that we use in volatile memory rather than going to all the trouble to translate it into forms suitable for storing in slow, magnetic storage. Even if the power failed the information would be there, exactly as we left it, when the computer restarted.

There are various high-speed persistent memory technologies being worked on. I'm sure that they will be available sometime in the next decade. As soon as that happens, the need for databases will disappear. The whole architecture of systems will change to saving-memory structures that are immediately usable by programs.

At that point there will be no point in criticizing relational databases because they will become a relic of past technology, and enterprise systems will be much improved because of it. In fact, any kind of database, including the newer NoSQL[24] databases, will become obsolete. I, for one, can't wait. For programmers it will be totally liberating, and for users it will make systems, including enterprise systems, faster to implement, more reliable and much, much cheaper.

---

[24] Many programmers have become so disgusted with relational databases that they have developed more modern database types that are collectively referred to as NoSQL. When you name something as not being something else it is never a compliment. Think non-toxic, anti-viral or unleaded.

15
THE ENTROPY DEATH SPIRAL

When a star runs out of fusion, components that generate its immense outpouring of energy, it starts to collapse under the force of gravity. The force of gravity increases as the diameter gets smaller, and hence the collapse gains speed. If the star is large enough there is no known force in the universe that will stop it from collapsing down to a single point and becoming a black hole. A black hole sucks in any matter that comes close and lets nothing out, including light.

Entropy in an enterprise system is like the force of gravity. It feeds on itself. As the entropy in a system grows, the rate of entropy growth increases. This is an exponential growth rate and it can spell death for a system.

As the code is more disordered and programmers are swapped in and out of the project, the entropy grows. Badly-commented code, badly-named subroutines, human errors—all of these contribute to problems. When programmers new to the project start working on the code they are much more likely to make mistakes because of their unfamiliarity with the fixing and patching that has already occurred. This of course increases entropy.

The programming team misses deadline after deadline and is subject to intense pressure to get things working. This pressure causes stress which, of course, increases entropy, as the programmers are the only conduit for code to enter the system. Stress also accelerates turn-over of the project team as members burn out or take other jobs to get away from the toxic environment. As we have discussed, turnover of project staff is a major contributor to project entropy.

This situation now feeds back on itself. As the entropy increases, the stress increases, which means more entropy. Stress creates more errors, which adds yet more entropy. Just like the gravity of a collapsing star, it grows exponentially.

It eventually gets to the point where finding and fixing the bugs exceeds the capability of humans to deduce the causes.

The system collapses into entropy death.

This is yet another way to conceive of entropy—as a black hole that just sucks in more and more of the system until it become totally unusable.

Scientists are interested in the symptoms of a star about to collapse, and the mechanisms that occur in a moment-by-moment analysis of the actual collapse. We, too, can look at the symptoms of the start of enter-prise system collapse.

SYMPTOMS OF AN APPROACHING ENTROPY COLLAPSE

How do you tell if a system is approaching an entropy meltdown? Unlike physical systems, entropy is largely invisible unless you are a programmer and have full access to the source code.

However, there are four definite symptoms of entropy growing out of control:

IS THE PROJECT TEAM UNDER STRESS?

Are there tensions in the team caused by system prob-lems? How is management handling this? Are they push-ing programmers to do more and do it faster?

These are all pretty obvious indications that there is trouble in the project and that entropy is growing.

IS THERE HIGH TURNOVER IN THE PROJECT TEAM?

This can be easily checked. If you are trying to assess a project, conduct exit interviews. Ask programmers why they are leaving. Get an honest assessment from programmers about the state of the project by making sure their remarks are confidential and will only be used for determining the project state and are not used for employee evaluation.

ARE THERE ANNOUNCED DATES FOR COMPLETION THAT ARE NOT MET?

Is there date, which will definitely be met, and then is missed? Is this happening time and again?

The Phoenix payroll system went through a series of these dates. The minister in charge announced that it would definitely be fixed by October 31, 2016—absolutely, definitely. It wasn't. The next date was the end of 2016. That went by with even more problems appearing. Then it was May 2017. That was not met either. After that it became difficult to determine the latest date. No doubt management was getting wary of being publicly embarrassed by announcing deadlines that weren't met.

This is a clear sign of a possible approaching system collapse. Management always wants to know some kind of completion date. The fact that no one actually knows what that date is, and the fact that it is not humanly possible to determine it, is not acceptable to most managers. So, programmers and project leads give the best number they can. They think about the issues they are facing and how long those kinds of things took in the past. They add all that up and throw in as much contingency as they think they can get away with. In other words, the date they produce is more about what is acceptable than what is real.

The reality is that no one knows. Because of NLP one of those small issues could balloon into a major time-consuming task. If the system has high entropy then starting all that activity can cause even more problems, each one of which can billow into something unpleasant. NLP has no respect for past history. Even if you solved similar problems hundreds of times before, it is possible that the subtle differences in this particular case will make all your past experience completely irrelevant. Of course, high-entropy systems make estimations even harder and even more meaningless.

Programmers keep on giving dates, which are usually made more optimistic by sales teams before being presented to a customer. The fact that these dates are usually nonsense is not something that management wants to hear. This is because most management is stuck in that physical world mindset. They are used to getting fairly reliable estimates when it's a physical project. Sure, they go over budget, but once any unforeseen obstacles have been overcome, the estimates of time-to-complete are pretty good. Management assumes that if the programmers are skilled professionals then they should be able to perform at that kind of level. As we now know, it doesn't work this way in the software world.

However, the one thing I have noticed with software estimates is that if the project is under control then the estimates of the time to complete start to get smaller. Even though the dates are not met the slippage is always around the size of the estimate. In other words, if the estimate is a year then we are talking years, if it is a month we are talking months, so when we get down to days it is indeed getting close.

On the other hand, a project that is high entropy and spinning out of control will keep on having estimates that keep on being missed; instead of converging they just keep happening at the same scale. This is a sign that programmers are feeding management what they want to hear. They know if they say a year the executives may have simultaneous heart attacks. So, they say six months and, even though management fulminates and pounds the table, they accept it. The next time they are asked to explain why the deadline wasn't met and when it will absolutely, definitely be finished, the programmers give the same kind of time scale as the previous estimate, based on their feeling of what will be accepted. This means that the estimates are always for six months longer, or whatever number management seems to accept. Unlike a project in control, the estimates don't converge down to smaller and smaller time scales, they continue being the same.

DO NEW ERRORS KEEP APPEARING?

There are errors in all software, and it is only testing that gets rid of enough of them to reach something usable. At first the testing team finds errors faster than they can be fixed, but after a while, if the project is in some kind of control, more bugs are fixed than are found. In this scenario the list of unfixed bugs shortens as fewer bugs are discovered. Another indicator of a project under control is that as the testing continues, newly discovered bugs are less severe.

Alternatively, if the project is starting to collapse under the weight of its entropy, new errors will keep appearing and some of them will be major defects. In fact, in an entropy collapse the number of bugs found per day keeps increasing while the number of bugs fixed per day decreases.

THE INTERDEPENDENCE OF BUGS

One characteristic of an out-of-control system is that it starts to depend on bugs to function. As programmers desperately try to fix problems, they fix them in ways that rely on other bugs to work.

Suppose one part of the software is flipping the sign of a number. For example, 500 is being wrongfully turned into a negative number, -500. There could be thousands of lines of code that are working to produce the number. Where is the problem? This is not theoretical, as the sign of a number can be disagreed upon by different parts of software. Normally in enterprise systems credits are represented by negative numbers and debits by positive ones. However, we know that in a payables report the credit amounts of the invoice are displayed as positive and the payments which are debits to the accounts payable account are negative. This is because the report is stating the amount the organization owes and the payments reduce that amount. We naturally want that amount to be positive and the reducing quantities to be negative.

This means that there are different contexts in the system where signs are flipped. It might be that a routine is passing back the payable amount instead of the G/L amount.

And in the spirit of entropy combing with entropy, it may be that the code is so hacked up with misleading names, misleading comments, and misleading instructions, that you cannot find the source of the problem.

I know this sounds a bit odd to non-programmers. "Surely," you may be thinking, "you can trace it down to the cause of the sign flip." What you need to do is have some test data that exhibits this problem, and then debug through the code to try to see where its operation diverges from what you expect. But the code is thousands of lines, full of subroutine calls. That means you have to look down in the subroutines to see if they are the cause, but they can call other subroutines, which in return can call still other subroutines. In some parts of the software this can descend 20 or 30 levels. If you can run a debugger then you can insert "break points" in the code to stop at certain points, and then you can try to determine what is going wrong. But where do you set the break point? Can you catch the error as it happens? If this is high-entropy source code, i.e. confusing, convoluted, and sometimes just plain dumb, then it may be near impossible.

Sometimes you cannot run a debugger, or perhaps the error doesn't appear when you do. Then you are forced to use debugging dumps, which are text messages sent to a console display. By displaying the value of certain memory locations you can try to understand what is happening. This means that you have to try to determine what values you should display, which means that you have to understand the bug enough to figure out the relevant information. Invariably you never get this right the first time, and it takes many tries, each time changing the program and rebuilding the system. If the system is in a high-entropy state, with badly written code that has been hacked and slashed to make it work, it can be essentially impossible to figure out in any kind of reasonable time.

Even if you find the place where the sign is being changed, is it the only place? Even if you think you find the error in a high-entropy system you have the worry that changing that code is going to break other parts of the system.

Given project deadlines and pressure by management to "just make it work" programmers are tempted to just flip the sign back to what it should be and get on with it.

That may have to occur in many places, i.e. every time the number is used in another part of the calculation.

The result of this is that the proper working of the system now depends on that bug. If some other programmer later goes into that code and fixes the original bug, all the code that was fixed by reversing the sign will now fail. What happens is that the system starts to move into states where it is dependent on various bugs. The flipping of a sign is pretty obvious but they can get much subtler.

Bugs are like organisms and follow the "survival of the fittest" rule. Easy bugs are fixed quickly. Over time you are selecting for harder and harder bugs. Just as in evolution, you are selecting for bugs that have survival mechanisms. There are bugs that only show themselves when your debugger is turned off, and there are bugs that only happen at random times so it is near impossible to catch them in the act. There are bugs that only show in production runs but not the test runs. There are co-dependent bugs that only show up when two specific bits of code are run at the same time. These are just a few of the possible survival characteristics that allow a bug to evade detection and elimination. This is software, which is logic, and the ways in which bugs can baffle you are infinite. Of course, NLP makes sure that it is difficult, if not impossible, to localize these issues to try to get some control, and NLP means that the impacts of these bugs can be spectacular.

These kinds of tricky bugs are all over the software in a high-entropy system and so the dependency on bugs can be far more complicated than just a sign flip. But in all these cases the high-entropy software starts to build in dependencies on these bugs. Programmers rush in to fix problems and do something that looks promising. If it works they think, great, I've fixed it—but it could be a fix that is depending on another bug to work. When that bug is fixed or changed by another programmer, that other fix stops working and the problem reappears in some kind of form.

So now you have parts of the system that are not functioning, i.e. they have bugs, and other parts of the system that function but depend on the bugs in the first part. These dependencies can become mutually dependent; one part of the code depends on a bug in another but that other part of the code depends on the first part. This then becomes a game of "whack-a-mole." When you fix one bug the other part of the code starts producing errors. If you fix that one the first bug reappears.

This is almost impossible to control. The best you can hope for in these circumstances is some kind of managed stability.

This leads us to Zombie systems.

ZOMBIE SYSTEMS

Our school board in Vancouver is running a payroll system that is the same one that the Phoenix system is derived from. In this case, despite massive problems, the system has not been cancelled. It has been announced that it will take $850,000 dollars a year to keep the system running.

This kind of massive support is the indication of a zombie system.

Zombie systems are high-entropy systems that are used but are always on the edge of disaster. They take a team of programmers continually working on them just to keep them running.

They are the living dead.

You may have had experience with a zombie system, indeed your organization may be using one.

Zombie systems have continual problems. Each month there are different ones. The team works to fix each as it occurs. These are high-entropy systems that are on the edge of spiraling down to entropy death. It is always a struggle to keep this from happening.

Zombie systems don't tend to generate the same headlines as a total failure. When a system is abandoned it is much harder to keep it secret, especially if you are a public institution. Zombie systems on the other hand can have their outrageous operational costs factored into organizational budgets.

ENTROPY DEATH

Entropy death is the final stage of a high-entropy system. After becoming a zombie system if the entropy buildup is unchecked, i.e. if a massive amount of effort is not applied to keep the system running, it will descend into a non-working state. At this point there are so many errors that the system is to all intents and purposes useless.

It may not be possible to save a zombie system from drifting into entropy death. High-entropy systems are continually generating more entropy and the buildup may become such that a descent into entropy death is like being pulled down by a black hole—once you get into its grip there is no coming back.

One significant sign of impending entropy death is that the system just will not stabilize. Errors pop up and despite the project team's efforts, putting them down just seems to create other errors. If the errors are just too egregious to bear, the client will put a stake through the zombie's heart by cancelling the project.

But killing a system is not the end of the problems. Now we look to see how the ghost of a system can still wreak havoc long after the system has been killed.

16
THE GHOST OF ENTROPY DEATH

Tragically, Dave's brother Fred, who worked at the same government agency, had died[25]. This was just before the agency, tired of all the problems with their existing system, tried once more (I believe this was the third in a series of underperforming systems) to bring in a new software system.

As in a lot of system projects there was not a lot of thought given to converting the old data into the new system. Converting data is an unrewarding task. It usually requires a lot of mind-numbing code to read in data from the old system, transform it in various ways and export it into the new system. Quite often this is assigned to a junior programmer.

In the rush and panic of most systems there is not a lot of time for this so the conversion is done in the quickest and dirtiest way possible. This usually means not thinking about what data should be converted and what should not be, but just converting everything.

In the new system of the government agency all the previous employees, whether still working for the agency or not, were converted. This included Fred, Dave's recently departed brother.

Unfortunately, the way the system was constructed Fred's account couldn't be removed. Fred had been the

---

[25] These are made-up names. As I mentioned before I don't want to identify people or organizations involved in the negative circumstances of system problems.

initiator of many tasks and removing his user account would result in the deletion of a large number of important and ongoing work items. This meant that Dave had to be reminded of his dead brother every day. To add insult to injury, the software supplier charged the agency the per-seat fee for the deceased brother.

This is just what can happen when old, bad data is converted to a new system.

If the system is in entropy death like the Phoenix payroll system, things can go very badly for a replacement system. The trouble is that a lot of the problems can be in the data. It is very important that when transferring data from the old, broken system to the new system that problems are not transferred. Remember, entropy can be endlessly subtle in its effects. This means every bit of data has to be scrubbed, as if it was hospital equipment after a virus outbreak.

After three years of errors what state is the data in? How could you trust any of that poisoned data?

This is one of the problems with moving away from a system that has collapsed into entropy death. The data that the system has produced is totally untrustworthy. The high-entropy code will have produced a dazzling array of intricate bugs that have twisted and contorted the data so that it contains traps for anyone trying to use it.

If an organization just takes that data and tries to move on to a new system it will carry all those problems with it. This is the ghost of entropy death. Entropy not only kills systems but it attempts to creep into the new replacement systems via the data being converted.

This means that the data should all be extracted and verified. Any old data that is no longer required should be eliminated. But how to do this?

Every entropy death has its own characteristics so it is hard to give any general prescriptions. Let us look at the Phoenix system and examine how they might proceed so as not to fall into the same mess that they are trying to claw out of.

HANDLING HIGH-ENTROPY SOFTWARE

Taking the Phoenix payroll system as an example, I would recommend a manual phase that will allow the situation to be stabilized and each employee brought into a correct state. In these kinds of situations, you have to look at the volumes and decide what is practical. Manual processing for a temporary period of time is much more practical than a lot of managers would realize.

In the Phoenix case, for example, you only have 300,000 civil servants. It's a lot but if you get a team of 1,000 payroll clerks each one has to handle an average of 300 employees. Now probably most federal employees are on a salary basis and their payroll is straightforward. A person could put a spreadsheet together of their batch of 300 employees and enter in all the payroll history. Then they could manually calculate the payroll. This will allow each employee's case to be reconciled and allow any adjustments to be calculated. The checks can be written by hand.

It sounds clunky, and so un-modern, but it will work and can be implemented in a fraction of the time it will take to get a replacement system—and it will stabilize the current situation.

Doing a manual system optimizes what humans do best. They have the ability to handle and organize quickly a lot of different situations with unexpected twists. Computerized systems are really bad at this, they require a careful structuring of the data and processes. If you try to computerize chaos you get very fast-running chaos.

Once the situation is stabilized you can run the manual system indefinitely, albeit at a higher cost then a proper computer system. However, the auditor general had estimated the cost to fix the Phoenix system at 1.2 billion Canadian dollars. Now that is one of those phony numbers that no one really knows and so it's given to satisfy organizational perceptions rather than to be an accurate estimate of what the cost may be. In this case the auditor general doesn't want to suffer the embarrassment of having his estimate be woefully inadequate. So, unlike the cases of estimates being low-balled to avoid management fury, in this case the estimate was probably puffed up in an attempt to avoid under-estimation.

Whatever the reasoning behind that number, you can be certain it had no basis in any kind of reality as no human being can determine how long and what effort it will take to fix a system collapsing into entropy death. However, it does mean that the expectation for massive costs has been created, and the relatively minor cost of running a manual system would be much more acceptable.

The manual system allows the data to be thoroughly examined. Each employee should be asked to sign off on the accuracy of their pay, and the accuracy of their history which, of course, impacts pensions. At this point compensation can be paid for any issues caused by the Phoenix disaster. The result of this is that the data is totally cleaned and has the agreement of the employees that it is accurate.

While the manual system is being created and operated a new computerized system should be developed. This should not be the same kind of system that created this problem in the first place. It should be based on a payroll language that allows the government payroll staff to express the various payroll calculations even for complicated union contracts. This language should be in the terminology of payroll staff not of computer programmers. It should allow staff to describe the gross pay calculations either as fixed amounts per month or based on timesheets and an hourly rate. I have been working on this problem in my own research and I can say that it isn't easy, but I am convinced that is quite practical.

I believe that this approach is essential. For an organization as complex and varied as the Canadian Federal Government it just doesn't work to have payroll specialists try to describe things to programmers who then try to implement it. It will only work if the payroll staff can express the payroll calculations directly much as they would using a spreadsheet.

This new system should be tested relentlessly (remember it's all about the testing) so that the language is certified to be accurate. It is much easier to test a language than it is to test a customized system.

If this takes some time, and requires expert input, so be it. Once a manual system is running it allows time to get the next system right. If this development is late there is a measurable staff cost but no disaster. Manual systems can tolerate staff turnover much better than computerized ones can. If staff move on, the supervisors should be able to take over any batch of employees and assign it to another clerk as needed.

One necessary feature of the new system is that it must be able to display the logic tree that led to an amount being paid. In this way, whenever there is an issue over a payroll amount, the clerical staff can get a display of the calculation and see exactly how the computer arrived at that number and reconcile it with what the employee believes to be correct.

All of that said, I doubt that is what the government will do. It is a conservative and not very imaginative organization and will most likely follow the same script it uses when acquiring other systems. That means putting the system out for bid to the large software companies who have the resources to handle the expenses of bidding on and implementing large government contracts. Civil servants are usually reluctant to take an innovative approach, as they see it as high risk with possible negative consequences to their careers.

Given that the potential bidders have incredible failure rates in even straightforward implementations, it is very likely we will be hearing about the payroll woes of Canadian civil servants for years and years to come.

BEWARE

Let me repeat my advice here to anyone who is experiencing or has just experienced a system collapse. Beware the ghost of entropy death. Just because you start a new system doesn't mean you are out of the woods. Make sure you have a clear strategy that will allow you to go forward without dragging the ghosts of systems past with you.

17
SPEED OR ACCURACY

$154.34 a night—that was what the Airbnb website was showing. The trouble was it wasn't the amount the account holder had set and try as we could we could not reconcile it in any way to the various costs and exchange rates. Then when you reloaded the page it sometimes changed to another rate that also seemed to be close but not related to any of the other numbers.

I was helping an AirBnB host deal with the website. She was trying to figure out the various rates the site was displaying. I might know a few things about computer systems but I was of no particular help in this case. The website just kept on displaying numbers with no discernable reconciliation to any actual numbers in play.

Another issue concerned a bonus payment that was owed to the account but hadn't been paid. After several calls to the support line, AirBnB subtracted the bonus instead of adding it. When they finally corrected that they miscalculated the amount, overpaying by two hundred dollars and messing up the history of past transactions. At what point do you give up?

This is common behavior in large commercial web sites. Rather than fix the software they put a lot of effort into customer support. Support reps can examine the account and make manual corrections. The large number of customer support people this requires and the large number of technical staff needed to keep the high-entropy software running costs a lot of money.

Users are more likely to pursue complaints when underpaid rather than overpaid, so the company loses out on this kind of remediation. But if you have millions of customers all paying for your service, the income is so large that these mistakes are just a minor cost of business.

The rise of websites that provide a service to millions of people shows a different path to traditional software development. In these cases, time to market is often far more important than accuracy or maintainability. You can spend a long time designing and building software so that is low entropy, extensible, and scalable—by that time your competitor had been out for a year and is dominating the space.

In these cases, you build fast and try to get the MVP (minimal viable product) out as quickly as possible. This is a risky approach. Along the steep, rocky road to incredible riches are the bleached bones of many web platforms that went out of business. For a lot of them this happened because they couldn't make the resulting high-entropy codebase handle a massive increase in customers. These software considerations are a large part of the volatility of the software wild west that constitute today's web services industry.

These website services use browsers on the customer's desktop. A browser is just a program that will connect to websites and download information along with metadata about how to format and operate with it. You almost certainly use one of the five major browsers (Chrome, Firefox, IE, Edge, Safari) to visit websites.

That means that the software being used for these websites is a combination of the software on the server serving up the webpage, and the browser which is displaying it.

When you put this rapid development together with the entropy of having to support five different browsers that are built and supported by other organizations it becomes impossible to get completely accurate results.

But as mentioned, for this kind of software speed to market is more important than accuracy. The customer base is also huge and hence there are no large crucial customers whose problems have to be solved if the company is to stay in business.

One of Facebook's company values is "Move fast and break things." It's a new mantra for this kind of software development, and the tools being used to produce this software are incredibly flexible, dynamic, and high entropy.

What about this kind of approach being used for enterprise software? If you don't understand enterprise software you are liable to think one approach fits all and use these kinds of technologies for enterprise.

ACCURACY

I started doing enterprise systems by working closely with accountants. Accountancy has always been about accuracy and reliability. Being correct to the penny is not only a sign of being in control of the numbers but in double-entry book keeping it is a check on the consistency of the data.

In my early experience with enterprise systems it was drummed into me that things had to be accurate to the penny. Consequently, it has always been a goal for me to make the systems totally accurate.

I also hate having to do emergency fixes—the kind of emergency that starts with a call at 4 a.m. telling you that the whole system is failing and it needs to be fixed quickly. It's a lot of tension and fear, because it means trying to solve a problem under time pressure. I try to build my systems so that errors are easy to diagnose and repair. This means a lot of work on trying to find the right way to construct the system, it means a lot of thought into future extensions, and it means putting work into parts of the system that may not pay off until later.

This is the reverse of the kind of programming used for web and mobile technologies. There we saw that the winner is often the one who makes it first to the market regardless of a myriad of defects in the software.

Enterprise software is about accuracy and reliability. It is mission critical. You cannot have random errors and strange events. It is the realm of being exact. This means that the techniques used for mass web-based applications are just not sufficient for enterprise. Enterprise requires low entropy because there is going to be on-going maintenance. There are also going to be changes to the business rules as businesses evolve. If you have high-entropy code this will, as we have seen, lead to a continual series of difficult problems.

I point this out because there is so much hype and enthusiasm in the software world that business people are presented with the development tools of webservices and the programming techniques they use, as if they are the next great thing and will solve all their problems. Young programmers especially are given to thinking that the latest fad they have just learned is the way of the future and everything should be done that way. We are all zealots when we are young. Unfortunately, software has no respect for zeal and enthusiasm. It is a methodical task that takes discipline. Even with low-entropy code it can be bafflingly frustrating. Being forced to maintain high-entropy code is my idea of work hell.

All that said, it is also true the businesses today have to incorporate websites and mobile apps into systems. These websites and apps provide a way of communicating with clients, staff, and the general public that just cannot be done any other way. So how do you incorporate those technologies into your enterprise system and not have it sucked down into a whirlpool of entropy?

WEB AND MOBILE INTERFACES

One approach would be to develop the website or mobile app as a low-entropy code base. Unfortunately, that option is no longer really viable, because you pretty much have to use one of the standard frameworks, which are quick development but higher-entropy tools.

One of the issues for websites and mobile apps has been the bewildering array of devices they have to work on. All of the different screen sizes and different operating systems (mainly iOS and Android) have spurred the creation of development environments that can generate software that will work properly on all the different platform variations. These are often called "frameworks" and at the time of writing this they are all based on a language called JavaScript[26]. There is now too much work in trying to support all of these possibilities for an enterprise programming team. By using the framework, the programmers can gain the benefit of the framework code making all the necessary adjustments for the different platforms and screen sizes.

JavaScript is what is called a dynamic language. That means that the program that turns it into machine code doesn't heavily check that certain operations can be done

---

[26] JavaScript has no direct relationship to the other computer language called Java. JavaScript was originally called 'livescript' by its inventor Netscape. They changed the name to JavaScript because in the mid-1990s Java was the hot way of actually having a website you could interact with (they had all been just read-only info before this) and Netscape wanted to share some of this attention. After a while it became popular enough that it needed a standard. None of the common standard organizations really wanted to handle such a thrown-together language. The ECMA (European Computer Manufacturer's Association) took it on as a standard. Although it is popularly called JavaScript, it is officially ECMAScript.

to certain kinds of data. In comparison the Java language is very strict and won't pass anything that doesn't obey its rigid typing of data and what you can do to it. In JavaScript things go wrong when the program is running rather than when the program is being built.

Dynamic languages can be fast development but they are very high entropy. JavaScript has also been modified and added to extensively. JavaScript is currently at version 8. The language has changed from its simple roots to having very sophisticated software concepts that are very complicated and can produce subtle bugs that are near impossible to find.

This is one of the reasons that websites are chronically very late. If there is extensive JavaScript usage in a project it is going to be very hard to get it to stability.

Many developers will claim to be able to throw together this kind of software is a matter of days or weeks. They may get a working prototype up, but it takes much longer to get something that is actually useful. What they are doing is using the customer base as their QA department. Over time the website may become a somewhat reliable working site, but that will take a long time, and there will be many tears along the way.

So how do you separate the two and make sure the high entropy from those technologies doesn't leak into your low-entropy enterprise system.

This is done by using APIs. API stands for "Application Programming Interface." This is the standard way for programs to connect to third party or internal servers. Basically, a computer sends a text request that is a list of named values. The sender and receiver have to agree on what the names are and what the values mean. Usually this is all documented by the people who designed the server API.

For example, you might send text to UPS that has a value named "waybill number." Then UPS can send back tracking data in the agreed-upon format. Of course, you probably also had to send named values like "account id" and "password" with your request.

Enterprise systems have to offer such interfaces to mobile and web applications but even more than that they have to treat the mobile or website software as untrusted. This means they cannot depend on the data being correctly formatted or having correct values. If the app or website is open to the public there may be data that was constructed with malicious intent. It requires an extensive analysis of how to handle all the possible problems in the data. Extensive instrumentation is needed to be able to intelligently log all interactions and trace down incidents.

This can be done, but I stress that it takes care and attention to detail. If this is just fobbed off on a junior programmer to throw together an interface then the entropy of the outside world may seep into your enterprise system and cause problems.

18

FOUR TIPS WHEN GETTING A NEW SYSTEM

What can you do in the short term to improve your chances of getting a useful and efficient enterprise computer system for your organization?

As you have no doubt gathered by now, this is not an easy task. There is a lot that can go wrong with a computer system. But now you are forearmed with a deeper understanding of how these systems can go wrong.

Knowing this what can you do?

It does depend somewhat on whether your supplier is doing a custom build or customizing an existing system. Even a custom build will probably start with a bunch of already-existing code that handles common functions like identity and login, screen formatting, persistent storage and forms.

There are four tips for what you can do:

1. Limit project entropy.
2. Don't be misled by glitz.
3. Detect high entropy.
4. Negotiate cost based on your estimate of entropy.

TIP #1 – LIMIT PROJECT ENTROPY

There is a lot in a project that you have some say in, and you can get more if you demand it. One of these is project staff turnover. This is one of the biggest contributors to entropy. You should not block the removal of underperforming programmers, as bad programmers can have a negative effect on the project and removing them is a net positive. But you should resist any supplier trying to swap programmers in and out for other reasons. Some less scrupulous suppliers will put an A team in to get the business, and over time swap out the A programmers for less-experienced and less-knowledgeable Bs.

This is bad for obvious reasons but each of the programmers leaving is taking project knowledge with them. So even if they were replaced with equally-skilled programmers, the project will still suffer.

My observation has been that systems done by smaller companies with existing software or tools are the most likely to succeed. These tend to be smaller programming shops that have business software that they can modify or that use a language/environment that they are skilled in to build it from scratch. This tends to work better because:

1. They choose their clients more carefully because they are very aware of which situations they can handle and which they can't.

2. If they are modifying an existing codebase, they know it from bottom to top because they wrote it. They have a well-developed sense of what changes will have what impacts. If they are building from scratch they tend to have a realistic assessment of their capabilities, the capabilities of tools they are using, and what kinds of systems they can build.

3. They have a dedicated team that does one system at a time and hence they don't tend to swap programmers in and out of projects.

Going with a large company with a large advertising budget and lots of media attention may seem like the best bet, but in enterprise software it rarely is. You have very little leverage with such a company and they will tend to do what they want with your system.

TIP #2 – DON'T BE MISLED BY GLITZ

If you look at the websites for enterprise systems, especially those from large companies, they are really slick. Some of them are so well designed they look like car ads, with smooth, gleaming surfaces and immaculate color choices. They have images of smiling, multi-ethnic, and gender-balanced workers staring in awe at the magic information on a laptop. They claim that companies using their product have made more profit, and they back this up with glowing testimonials. There is, needless to say, no mention of colossal system failures. After all, if a client does have a problem it must be the client's fault.

Just because the software supplier is a large company don't take its competence for granted. Don't fall for the misconception that large companies are better at software than smaller ones. Remember, it will be human programmers who are customizing the system to your special needs. Large companies hire from the same pool as everyone else and their programmers are no better than anyone else's. So just because the company has a software system that has a huge marketing budget, we have seen in earlier chapters that the software doesn't bring much to the table if it has to be modified significantly.

I have been working on software to allow business people to set up their own systems and there is software by other companies that are attempting the same thing. If you can get software that will help your own staff build a system you will be much better off. Your staff understands your organization better than any consultant ever can.

TIP #3 – DETECT HIGH ENTROPY

There are certain external characteristics that indicate high-entropy code. You want to avoid ending up with a high-entropy code base at all costs. High-entropy code is very, very difficult to diagnose, fix, or modify.

It is the nature of entropy to grow. The more entropy, the faster it grows. You should think of entropy as a corrosive rust. When you introduce a high-entropy system you are dumping that corrosive rust into your organization and it will seep into different areas and negatively impact your operations.

Mistakes made by systems are carried into other systems. They introduce errors. For example, system crashes cause tension and stress which will cause people to make other errors. People will get frustrated if they have to battle a system. The stress makes them less effective and takes time away from important tasks.

To avoid high entropy, these are some of the things you should look for:

CAN THE MANUFACTURER EASILY CHANGE ALL THE NAMES IN THE SYSTEM TO FIT YOUR ORGANIZATION'S NOMENCLATURE?

Nomenclature is really important in organizations. Each organization develops names for things in its own way and those names are embedded in the corporate culture.

I have built many time-billing systems and each organization had a different name for a project. These included "project", "contract", "job", "task", and "test". The names for sub-projects included "sub-project", "sub-task", "division", "discipline", and "department". Using a different word than the one used commonly in the organization is extra entropy. Every time employees have to deal with system results they have to mentally translate the words. This is a simple thing but it adds a level of confusion and increases the chances of miscommunication.

You must think about what it means if a supplier cannot match your nomenclature exactly. It means that the names of things are randomly scattered throughout their code base. It is a symptom of high entropy. If they had well-organized and well-written software, then the names should be in a central place and easy to change.

If you are getting a custom build, then they should be able to make the system fit your organization like a glove. If they can't fit to your nomenclature then you should interrogate them to figure out why not. It could be that they are using inflexible tools that put too many strictures on their build and hence will produce a higher entropy system than is desirable.

CAN THE MANUFACTURER DELIVER A SYSTEM THAT MEETS YOUR NEEDS AND HAS NO UNUSED FEATURES?

Remember that features you don't use cost you money. They introduce corrosive entropy into your organization. They are of no use to you and are just accidents waiting to happen. They clutter up your system interface and make it harder to use. You have to train people to ignore this button, that menu choice, and all those columns on a screen.

These features are not for your benefit, they are for the benefit of the manufacturer. They are trying to attract more clients with added features.

Consider the software that cannot have features easily removed. This means that the code is not well organized. If menu choices and buttons are randomly scattered throughout the code then what does that tell you about the way the code was designed and written? A lot of code is hacked and slashed over time to put in new features. Programmers implement new features and push them in anywhere they can. In a codebase like that it is very hard to turn off unneeded features because the programmers are not sure where to do that and what impact it will have on other code when they do.

All of this is high-entropy code and you should be very wary. If the supplier cannot remove all the unneeded features then this is a strong warning sign that this is a high-entropy codebase.

Your supplier may say that they are delivering a product and this is just the way it is. But, come on—this is the 21st century! Surely they can build the system so that it is easy to remove all the unnecessary features. The fact that they can't means that the code is high entropy and that they don't really care about your costs, they only care about their income.

If they are doing a custom build you should be able to get an exact fit to your organization with nothing extra. Don't fall for the claim that these features might be something you want in the future. Get the system you need now and deal with future features in the future. If they can't limit the feature set exactly to what you need then interrogate them carefully to determine why.

HOW ARE THEY GOING TO FIX BUGS?

Suppose, right at your peak business time the system starts dropping key information like orders. What is the process to find and fix the problem? How quickly are they going to respond? Do they have the ability to trace everything and diagnose a problem? Can they run a debugger on the operational code and watch what is happening? Do they have a well-designed event-logging strategy?

Too many systems are installed without any thought of instrumentation.

Recently in my province of British Columbia there was a report of a government system that crashed and the technical staff could not figure out why for several weeks. This was a $160,000,000 project. You would think that for that kind of money they would get decent instrumentation.

According to media reports, the system was combining data from several web sites. In those cases, there should be very strict checking of data and a conversion to a common format before data is let into the main part of the system. At all of these input nodes there should be logging and monitoring of the data flowing. The fact that they couldn't trace a system failure quickly shows that they had a badly-designed and high-entropy system. Of course, there was no question of retrieving any money.

Customers just seemed baffled by all of this and because they don't really understand the software, contracts are often written by the supplier. In that kind of scenario system failure is never the supplier's fault.

Another issue is how the code handles errors internally. This is a hard one for you to check without looking at the code but asking for it will reveal whether they have a coherent solution or whether it's just high-entropy time with every programmer making up how they handle errors.

If the code base is well-organized it should not be a problem to get back a succinct and rational description. You can then give it to a third-party expert and have them evaluate it. If the supplier has no strategy around these issues then they probably will resist giving you that information. You can draw your own conclusions from that.

CAN THEY EASILY RECONCILE RESULTS?

This is a something that you need to ask for. If they report a number, can they show where that number came from? This is more than the drill down you get in packaged accounting systems. That drill down is good, but you want something even more. If there is a number, you want to know how it was calculated and why it is that exact value.

I spent a lot of time once trying to figure out why Quicken was returning a certain answer. There was no way to show all of the settings that were impacting the result. After a long and frustrating few days it turned out it was an exchange rate that had been set and not updated. There was no way to get the system to explain why that number was exactly what it was. If it had been able to do that I would have immediately seen the problem.

In a payroll system you should be able to see for every employee exactly why the amount on the check is what it is. There should be a dump of the logic and data that went into the calculation. In that way if there is disagreement over the amount, the calculation can be followed step by step until the source of disagreement is identified.

These are ways you can challenge a software salesperson and get some insight into whether the code base is high entropy. Don't let them blow you off with technobabble. If they don't know the answers then have them bring in someone who does. You are a smart person and this stuff is not that difficult at this level.

Think of the software as an organization that you are investigating and trying to figure out if it is well organized or just a mess. Not being able to change nomenclature or remove unwanted features is a definite sign of disorganization. Press them on it. Why can't they?

Remember that technical people are usually more honest than salespeople about defects. They hate to say things that are technically incorrect—it just goes against their nature. You can get the best information by interviewing them alone, i.e. without a salesperson present. Don't let them descend into technicalities but keep them on the bigger picture and have them explain what they have to do to accomplish the things you are asking about. If you go through it carefully you can get a good picture of the state of the software without being an expert.

TIP #4 – NEGOTIATE COST BASED ON YOUR ESTIMATE OF ENTROPY

This is where you can exert pressure on a supplier. The cost of the software is very negotiable already. ERP companies give away massive discounts; 75% is not unheard off, just to get you to use the software. As expensive as this software is, the real money is in the per-seat and maintenance costs.

If you detect high entropy, challenge the salesperson on it. Push them on all issues. If they are willing to make concessions make sure you ask for reduced per-seat costs and reduced maintenance costs. After all, if this is a high-entropy code base then you are taking a significant risk in using it. There costs should reflect this risk. Just discounting the acquisition cost doesn't do it. The high-entropy nature of the software is going to be a continual expense and you should be recompensed on a continual basis.

If the salesperson refuses then perhaps you should look for a supplier who is more flexible in pricing so they can compensate for deficiencies.

SUMMARY

Selecting, implementing, and operating enterprise software is a difficult and risky task with today's technology. There is a tendency for business people to hide their heads in the sand because they don't really want to think of these complicated issues. This is a mistake. Computer software is becoming more and more important in organizations and hiding from the issues will just make things worse.

When it comes down to it, it's all about the programming team. If there is going to be customization work or a full custom development then you want to make sure you have a good, well-qualified team that is going to stay for your whole project.

It's hard for a non-technical person to judge programmers. If you are having an existing system modified then choose a company that still has the software creators working for it and is proud of its software. In that case you have a better chance of success.

If you are getting a full custom build then get a commitment that the team will not change. You can even introduce penalty clauses if there is turnover in the team. Remember every time there is a change in the team personnel it is a cost to the project. Make sure that any such personnel changes require your approval.

19
LONG TERM

One day in the mid-1970s I arrived at the office in the middle of the morning. I had been up late the night before as it had been the month end. We had a Prime[27] minicomputer that I had acquired and programmed to do the company's accounting. The system combined input from the branches across the country and produced all the financials and management reports.

Despite phoning and pushing it always took a long time to get all the branches closed off so that we could start the month-end run which took all night. We were on the west coast so that gave the eastern branches extra time before the deadline but it was always late in the evening when my team finally got to turn things over to the night operator and we were able to go home. So it was 10 a.m. or so when I arrived, and the reports had already been distributed and were being examined by the accountants and executives.

I grabbed a cup of coffee and wandered down the hallway to the corporate controller's office. I found him and the CFO puzzling over one of the reports. In the general ledger there had been a transfer from the head office account to the Edmonton branch that they couldn't explain.

---

[27] Prime was one of the smaller mini computer manufacturers. They were part of a group of seven mini computer manufacturers that were challenging IBM, who had most of the market. Collectively they were known as the 'seven sisters.' They have all gone bankrupt or been swallowed up by more current technology firms.

We looked into it and it became clear that it was the result of a new policy that head office had introduced. In this company the branches were profit centers and totally responsible for all costs and incomes. The head office had decided to charge interest on work in progress (WIP). WIP is unbilled work, so you get it by subtracting the fees billed from the fees that had been generated but not yet billed. The head office reasoned that they were providing the financing for the WIP and hence it would be fair to collect interest. This would encourage branches to speed up billing and hence collections.

What had happened was that Edmonton had negative WIP. The reason for this was that they were doing a lot of prebilling for projects, so in this month their billing exceeded the work they had done, and the WIP was calculated as negative.

I had implanted this new policy during the month by multiplying the WIP by the percentage and crediting that amount to the branch and debiting that amount to the head office.

This meant when the WIP turned out to be negative the product was negative and hence the debits and credits switched and the money went the other way.

When it became clear what had happened it started a discussion that involved the CEO. The corporate controller told me that they hadn't intended to pay interest when the WIP went negative, and he had just taken that for granted. He was an accountant and I was a mathematician. To him calculating the interest didn't imply that it should be done for a negative amount. To me it was just an equation and the amount to transfer was the WIP times the percentage. It didn't occur to me to ignore negative WIP.

The discussion became a bit political. By making all the branches profit centers the company had done very well. The branches were run efficiently and each took full advantage of local conditions. The counter to this was that the branch managers couldn't be directly told what to do and still be expected to have full responsibility for profit. Also, they were part of the employee ownership so they were very powerful in the company.

By now the Edmonton branch manager had seen the reports and would not look kindly at the head office reducing the profit number that his and his staff's bonuses were based on.

The decision was to leave it. All the executives agreed that if it was logical to charge interest for financing WIP it was logical to pay interest on any branch that managed to bill before doing the work and hence in effect was contributing to the financing of other branches. Besides, that decision removed the necessity of reversing out some of the Edmonton branch's profit.

I can remember at the time walking away from the meeting thinking how my code had changed company policy—company policy was now what was in the code not necessarily what the organization had decided on. I remember clearly a shock of realization that this was going to become very common, that software was going to play a large part in determining corporate policy that was actually used as opposed to what management might believed was being used or wanted to be used. Since then I have seen many incidents where an enterprise system produced results that the staff couldn't really reconcile and weren't what they wanted but were forced to accept because no one knew how to correct it.

That was a cold shock of realization that the future might not be as technologically perfect as I thought in those days. However, at the time I didn't realize something bigger— that computerization of businesses represented the first time in the 11,000 years since the invention of accounting

217

by the Sumerians in Mesopotamia, that the accountants in an enterprise didn't understand and weren't totally in control of every step involved in the production of the corporate accounts and management information.

Before this company introduced a computer and had me program a system, this would never have played out this way.

In the previous era the calculations were done by clerical staff. The corporate controller would have ordered a journal entry for each branch, transferring the interest. He would review those entries and see immediately that there was a transfer where the debit and credit were reversed. Actually, the clerk preparing the journal entry and doing the multiplication would no doubt bring it to his attention as an unusual situation.

The point here is that before the advent of computers the corporate controller totally understood his system. As was common in that era, he came up through the ranks working in the accounts payable department, the accounts receivable department, and preparing financial reports. He had actually participated in those calculations and knew the procedures of each of those departments thoroughly. Even during the semi-automated era of unit record equipment (punched cards) the technology was really just a fast way of doing the accounting calculations that the accountants designed. In that era the corporate controller would be the one implementing the CFO's requirements.

That incident about the interest showed that he didn't understand the working of the system. He had to take my word for what it did and what it would do in the future. He wasn't a programmer and couldn't understand the logic that I had implemented in the code, as it was in one of those hyper-technical standard computer languages[28].

---

[28] It was in COBOL as I remember it.

This lack of understanding by accounting and operations staff created the need for an intermediary, the IT department. Instead of actually being in charge of the implementation of business systems, accountants now had to request features and consequently lost any understanding of what the impacts of new features would be. They were relegated to the role of consumers of a service without real control over how the service was constructed. Accountants could be told that a feature they wanted was not practical to be implemented in the current system, and they had no real way of evaluating that opinion let alone contesting it.

This is where the rubber hits the road. Businesspeople, mainly unknowingly, made a Faustian bargain, trading their understanding of the systems for the power of computerized information processing.

This produced a situation where businesspeople have to explain their needs to technical staff who then convert what they understand of these needs into system code. Technical staff are swamped with technical issues and don't have either the time or the experience to really understand the business issues. To counter this another layer in this information communication chain has been added—business analysts. These are business people who are more technically aware than the operational staff and hence can talk to both sides. This becomes like the game of "party-line," where a message is whispered from person to person. Everyone laughs when the totally distorted message is reported by the last person.

In the future we have to get to the state that businesspeople understand their systems as they did the human systems of the past.

There has been a rise of new titles in corporations, such as Chief Information Officer (CIO) and Chief Data Operator (CDO). The question is whether these are real positions or just temporary constructs that were created because of the unfamiliarity with new unreliable technologies?

At the turn of the 20th century the technological boom was electrification. It is hard for us to imagine now what a revolution this was, but previously power was dispensed mechanically by pulleys connected to rotating shafts, all driven by a steam engine. This meant that the positioning of equipment on the machine floor was dictated by having to have it positioned beneath the appropriate rotating shaft. When electricity came in it made it possible to position equipment to make production more efficient rather than constrained by the power source. Wires could be run virtually anywhere.

However, the starting stages were not that easy. This conversion was in some ways similar to the conversion from paper to computer. This newfangled electricity was an invisible power source, unlike the obvious transmission of power with belts, pulleys, and rotating shafts. There were strange rules about how many motors could be driven off a circuit; power sources were unreliable, with blackouts, brownouts, and power surges that caused problems in crudely-wired equipment. Electric motors were often badly wound and short circuits were common. In the early days it required electricians to turn equipment on and off. In those circumstances a Chief Electricity Officer can seem sensible.

The question is does a CIO and those other positions really bring anything to the table? Or are those positions just an artifact of immature technology?

The accounting department has always been, until recently, the department that keeps track of how the organization is performing, and supplies management with all the information they need to run the organization.

Let us imagine that enterprise system technology has progressed to the point that electrical technology has reached after starting so primitively over a hundred years ago.

What would that look like?

It could be that you just ask for what you want, just as a senior executive would have asked when all the work was done by human assistants.

"Give me a pie chart of our sales by region and send it to all the sales managers."

"Generate a balance sheet for each department and then produce a grid that shows all the departments and the standard ratios for each."

You can see that there is no mention in those commands of networks, communications, PDFs, or other file types, whether it should be delivered to mobile phones, or how recipients of the data have to identify themselves—nothing of any of those thousand technical issues that keep CIOs in their C-suite jobs.

So just like today when we take electricity for granted and command it by flipping switches and plugging in equipment, in the future enterprise computing will be taken for granted and used without thinking about it. After all we don't want the technology, we just want the results.

This means that all of those job titles will disappear and will be regarded as just as quaint as the executives in charge of electrification in the start of the 20th century.

The only sane organizational structure is to have a single department in charge of all reporting and measurement of the organization's performance. An organization will always need financial statements prepared by accountants, so the single department will be the accounting department.

As I said earlier this is the first time in 11,000 years that the accounting department has lost control of some of these activities. It makes no sense organizationally to split these functions into multiple departments unless the technology is so primitive that it requires domain experts to operate. We should all look forward to a time when we can abandon these artificial titles and consolidate once more into a rational organizational structure.

How are we going to achieve the consolidation and rationalization of automated activities in an organization?

The key is "understandability".

UNDERSTANDABILITY

In the 1970s I was working for Computer Sciences Corporation (CSC) in Vancouver. We had the ground floor of a building and ran a remote data terminal to a Univac 1107 in Calgary. This was in the days when computers were massively expensive, and there wasn't enough business in Vancouver to justify having an actual computer on site. The oil patch in Calgary had a huge demand for computer processing of their seismic data, so the computer was located there.

We had a computer room with a machine the size of two or three freezers that incorporated a communications unit, a card reader, and a printer. Clients would submit a card deck to our operator and the results would be transmitted back to our printer in an hour or so.

For people who wanted to wait for the results we had a waiting room and provided some rather bad office coffee.

Every month an elderly gentleman would drive his old green Ford Galaxy into our parking lot. He came into our office dressed very neatly in a slightly threadbare gray suit and thin out-of-fashion tie. He was working for a software company that had "financial planning" software and was running a model for the Hudson Bay Corporation, which ran a lot of department stores in western Canada. The model was a basic consolidation of budgets, calculating percentages and summing up all the stores in the region.

He would give the card deck to our operators and then sit in our waiting room reading a paper and drinking our bad coffee until the results were ready and he drove back to his office.

This was considered complicated software. After all, it was a financial model and it required programmers to set it up and programmers to format the data so it could be read by the software. It was very expensive to run. Clearly, having enough income to pay for the elderly gentleman to deliver it in person and wait for the results meant that this was an expensive program. Just to consolidate the results over a few dozen stores cost many thousands of dollars every time.

If you had said that average businesspeople would do this one day by themselves, people would have said you were crazy.

Then they invented spreadsheet software.

Now that kind of consolidation is considered to be a trivial spreadsheet application. Almost all business-people can operate spreadsheets. The idea of paying thousands of dollars to consolidate several worksheets is ludicrous.

Just because something is considered technically com-plicated and in the realm of expensive programmers doesn't mean that it will be in the future.

This is what you, the businessperson, should be push-ing the industry to develop for enterprise computing. At the start of this chapter I told of the time when I realized that this had been lost.

This should be our goal. To figure out how we can build systems that are understood by regular people in business-es so they can design, operate, and maintain them. This is a goal I have been working towards for the last 15 years[29]. At present my conclusion is that there will be an intermediate stage where people of a skill set similar to business analysts can do all the systems work. This will remove one level from the communications chain which will automatically improve results. Eventually this kind of understanding can be transferred to non-technical accounting staff. If we can come to some commonly-accepted model, then we can train people in business schools to use this kind of software much as we train people in spreadsheets today.

I think accountants have to take a lead in this. They seem to have been pushed aside in corporations by IT. As I have said it makes no sense to have more than one department responsible for measuring and reporting on the organization. However, this will only happen if accountants start to become more assertive as to their role.

We have to get out of the mess we are in. I believe this can only be done if the users of the software, I'm looking at you dear reader, get a common vision of what they want. So far, they have had no idea of even what to ask for. If, as a group, they demand more understandable software it could start moving the industry in the right direction.

SUMMARY

In the near term I cannot see enterprise software changing. Large software companies have an entrenched and profitable position in a field full of total confusion. They are not going to give this up without a fight. The fact that they are causing a massive trauma to businesses is not as important to them as the fact that they are making immense profits.

I am sure that reason will eventually prevail and the present technologies that have caused so much confu-

---

[29] I have developed Formever software which incorporates all of my ideas of what software we need.

sion and devastation will be abandoned. There are already some small signs of this in the movement away from relational databases.

AI (artificial intelligence) is often mentioned as the future in enterprise computing. There have been articles saying that AI will replace accountants and start making sophisticated business decisions. I really doubt that this will happen anytime soon, and perhaps not in the first half of this century. After all we can't seem to do even a simple thing like pay people properly. It is hard to see how adding the complexity of AI to the current mess will make things any better. I think we have to straighten out our current problems and develop 100% reliable systems that produce 100% accurate information before we start down such a technically difficult road.

On the other hand, I do think that if systems are built correctly then we can grow AI on an assistant basis. Just like any worker that starts at a company, I think we start with simple requests and then see if we can build them into more complex operations. This all takes an underlying language that we can instruct the AI in.

This will not be easy and I'm not sure if accountants, after decades of being pushed aside by IT, have the will to try to reclaim their position. They have the power, as they are the ones who are certified and given statutory recognition. However, when I look at a lot of companies I see that accountants have withdrawn to just producing the financial reports and are no longer as important in organizations.

As I have said, I think that there will eventually be one department for these activities and it will be accounting. Given that accountants, from my anecdotal observations, do not seem to want to fight for this role it will probably be a long time coming.

20
CONCLUSION

Well there you have it. What I have written is my view of what is going on in enterprise systems and why enterprise systems fail so often.

I doubt that things will change anytime soon. There is too much money being made in enterprise software for software companies to want to change their approach. Indeed, why should they? Systems that take a long time to implement are money makers. The hourly rates are high and multiplied by a large number of hours they make marketing managers in these companies drool in anticipation. It is not only the implementation but also the ongoing maintenance. Zombie systems are hugely profitable as they just keep on generating those hourly charges year in and year out. Even systems that are somewhat stable will require changes whenever the inevitable changes to the organization happen, and that will generate even more revenue. Those changes may tip the system over into becoming a zombie, which is even more profitable.

That is perhaps overly cynical but I have seen much in this industry over the years that doesn't give me a lot of faith in the short term. However, over the medium term I am more of an optimist. I think it is possible to get systems that can be built by regular business people just as they set up systems in the pre-computer era. This along with the development of non-volatile fast memories will transform the whole enterprise software system.

Over my career I have become more and more embarrassed by the performance of my industry. If you mention enterprise software to people they usually wince. Their experience has been almost uniformly negative. This makes me ashamed of what we have done and I feel responsible for the pain inflicted on business by our clumsy technology over the last six decades.

I hope we can develop the technologies that will cause people to forget about enterprise systems and just use them, just as they do electricity or plumbing.

We have a lot of work ahead of us.

ABOUT THE AUTHOR

Dr. Lance Gutteridge has a Ph.D. in computability theory from Simon Fraser University (1972). He has taught mathematics and computer science at York University, Simon Fraser University and University of British Columbia. He has worked extensively on enterprise computer systems having written many time-billing systems, accounting systems, inventory systems, and a large variety of other enterprise applications.

He has worked in software in aerospace, languages, operating systems, engineering, and many other areas. This combined with Dr. Gutteridge's theoretical background gives him a unique perspective on the problems of software development and enterprise system development in particular.

In 1998, he and his business partners sold Paradigm Development Corp. which wrote software for large software companies like Microsoft and Adobe. Since then he has written fiction books, taught Java programming internationally, and researched enterprise system development.

Having been frustrated for decades with the tools available for enterprise system development he decided to tackle the problem head on. In 2004 he founded Formever Inc. to develop software that allows business people to develop enterprise software. He has been working for the last 14 years as CTO of Formever to produce working software that accomplished this goal.

FORMEVER™ SOFTWARE

As Dr. Gutteridge contemplated writing a series of books about the software industry, he realized that people would wonder if he could actually point to a valid alternative. "Talk is cheap. Show me the code," said Linus Torvald, inventor of Linux. So, Dr. Gutteridge set about creating Formever, an open-source tool that would allow people to create custom applications for their enterprise without having to code, because code would be handled "behind the scenes."

Formever is a Domain Specific Environment (DSE) for business. Within this environment business people can use drag-and-drop design tools, custom-defined values, selection lists, built-in procedure tools, simple report builders, and other easy-to-use tools to make a custom system that meets their own requirements, simply, quickly, and affordably.

In accordance with the design principles Dr. Gutteridge identifies in his book, Formever is low entropy and minimizes the effects of non locality and proportionality (NLP). Formever is a blank page on which business people can create the system they need, with a simple set of tools. It is free of preconceptions about how people run their business, so that everyone is free to do it their own way. This means localization for anywhere in the world, from Bangladesh to Bangor, Maine, is no problem. Multiple languages, multiple currencies, and multiple users in multiple locations are all possible, for companies of all sizes.

The intention is to liberate companies world wide from the hidden tax of unnecessarily complex IT. Think of the transformation in the business world with the advent of spreadsheet software like Excel, or presentation software like PowerPoint. When easy-to-use tools free business people to create according to their own visions, all sorts of new things become possible. Formever is the first shot of a revolution, finally proving that it is possible for enterprise software to be readily available, affordable, and suited to the purpose at hand.

Go to www.formever.com to see the code.

CONTENTS

www.ingramcontent.com/pod-product-compliance
Lightning Source LLC
Chambersburg PA
CBHW071240050326
40690CB00011B/2199